GLOBETROTTER
TRAVEL GUIDE

KRUGER NATIONAL PARK

D0569990

L.E.O. BRAACK

NH
NEW
HOLLAND

GLOBETROTTER

TRAVEL GUIDE

*** Highly recommended
** Recommended
* See if you can

First edition published in 1996
by New Holland (Publishers) Ltd.
London • Cape Town • Sydney • Singapore

24 Nutford Place
London W1H 6DQ
United Kingdom

80 McKenzie Street
Cape Town 8001
South Africa

3/2 Aquatic Drive
Frenchs Forest, NSW 2086
Australia

Copyright © 1996 in text: L.E.O. Braack
Copyright © 1996 in maps: Globetrotter Travel Maps
Copyright © 1996 in photographs:
Individual photographers as credited
Copyright © 1996 New Holland (Publishers) Ltd

ISBN 1 85368 570 4

Managing Editor: Sean Fraser
Editor: Susannah Coucher
Sub-Editor: Laurence Lemmon-Warde
Design Concept: Neville Poulter
Design and DTP: Sonya Cupido
Cartography: Globetrotter Travel Maps
Reproduction by Hirt & Carter (Pty) Ltd, Cape Town
Printed and Bound in Hong Kong by South China
Printing Company (1988) Limited

Photographic Credits:
Archival material, page 17; **Anthony Bannister**,
page 16; **L.E.O. Braack**, pages 6, 7, 13, 14, 15, 29, 30,
34, 37 (top), 41, 48, 57 (middle), 58, 62, 68, 71, 72, 73,
75, 78, 83, 84, 85, 87, 92, 97, 99, 100, 101, 102, 103;
Michael R. Brett, pages 8, 9, 11, 12, 13, 19, 21, 23, 25,
26, 27, 28, 31, 36, 37 (bottom), 38, 39, 40, 42, 43, 44, 45,
46, 47, 53, 54, 57 (top), 59, 60, 61, 64, 67, 69, 70, 74, 86,
88, 89, 96, 98 (top); *courtesy of* **Conservation
Corporation**, page 107 (top & bottom), 108, 111;
Nigel J. Dennis, cover (bottom left) [ABPL], pages 4
[SIL], 10 [SIL], 56 [ABPL], 80 [SIL], 82 [SIL], 90 [SIL],
95 [SIL], 98 (bottom) [SIL]; **Du Plessis** [PHOTO
ACCESS], page 104; *Getaway*/**D. Rogers**, cover
(top right, bottom right) *Getaway*/**D. Bristow**,
page 76 [PHOTO ACCESS]; **Walter Knirr**, page 113;
courtesy of **Mala Mala**, page 110; **Photo Access**, page
104; **Peter Pickford**, page 81, 112 [SIL]; **Peter &
Beverly Pickford**, page 32 [SIL]; **Alain Proust**,
title page, page 109; **Lorna Stanton**, cover (top left)
[ABPL], page 114; **James Stevenson-Hamilton
Collection**, page 20; **Struik Image Library**, page 17.
[ABPL: Anthony Bannister Photo Library; SIL: Struik Image Library]

Although every effort has been made to ensure
accuracy of facts, telephone and fax numbers in this
book, the publishers will not be held responsible for
changes that occur at the time of going to press.

Cover photographs:
Top left: *Hikers pause to absorb the beautiful scenery on
the Bushman's Trail.*
Top right: *The African elephant finds refuge from
poaching and urban encroachment in the Kruger.*
Bottom left: *One of the highlights of a visit to the Park
is an exciting night drive.*
Bottom right: *The attractive Mopani Camp overlooking
a watering hole frequented by thirsty game.*
Title Page: *Watering holes are usually teeming with
game, especially in the dry winter months.*

CONTENTS

1
Introducing the Kruger National Park

The Kruger National Park is one of the most highly acclaimed national parks in the world. Its expanse is breathtaking: covering very nearly 20,000 km² (8000 sq miles) of undisturbed savanna, woodland, riverine forest and craggy mountain ranges, an area comparable to Israel, Wales (UK), or the US state of New Jersey. Kruger has an exceptionally rich mix of wildlife, including some 490 species of birds, 147 mammal species, 94 different reptile species, 33 types of amphibians and a magnificent array of at least 200 different kinds of trees.

In this sun-drenched remnant of primitive Africa, you can still enjoy the thrill of seeing massive herds of buffalo, elephant, zebra and others freely roaming through grass-covered plains. At night, seated in the flickering light of a camp-fire, your conversation could be interrupted by the dominant roar of lion and the haunting hoots of hyena. The bushveld atmosphere is all-pervasive. It soaks into you as you unwind and become part of this untarnished splendour. Memories are created each day. Scenes which you will carry with you for a lifetime!

To make this gem of wild Africa easier for you to reach, a sophisticated infrastructure has developed, allowing you a comfortable air or road trip, plus accommodation to suit all tastes and budgets. The Kruger Park is one of the top attractions bringing foreign visitors to southern Africa and, with the restrictions of the haunted Apartheid years now gone, more and more people are discovering the exhilarating experience of a journey back in time!

TOP ATTRACTIONS

*** **The Big Five:** elephant, rhino, buffalo, lion, leopard.
*** **Wildlife diversity:** unrivalled magnificence.
*** **Private hideaways:** according to choice.
*** **Wilderness trails:** with rustic base-camps.
*** **Drives:** guided bush drives and night drives.

Opposite: *One of the African elephant's few remaining strongholds, the Kruger supports over 7500 of these awesome creatures.*

THE LAND

Kruger is an elongated slice of land about 345km (214 miles) from north to south, averaging 54km (33 miles) in width. Most of its area consists of gentle, undulating plains. The entire eastern boundary, however, is formed by the sharply defined low mountains of the Lebombo range. Several major rivers drain the area, all flowing west-to-east, these being the Crocodile, Sabie, Olifants, Letaba, Shingwedzi, Luvuvhu, and Limpopo. Heavy demands on water in recent decades by industries to the west of Kruger have led to some of these rivers changing from permanently-flowing to seasonal rivers. The dramatic impact this has had on plant and animal life near to these rivers has been a cause of great concern for conservationists.

Generally, the northern half of the Park is dominated by mopane-veld (*Colophospermum mopane*) while the southern half comprises a rich mix dominated by knobthorn (*Acacia nigrescens*), marula (*Sclerocarya birrea*) and bush-willow (*Combretum spp.*). The lower third of the Park is fairly dense and therefore not very favourable to game-viewing but is the preferred area for some animals like rhino. The Central region has extensive rolling grassland inhabited by large numbers of game and predators, while the North, covering a vast area, tends to be a rather monotonous sea of mopane but good for viewing buffalo, elephant and some of the rarer antelope species such as Lichtenstein's hartebeest, sable, roan, eland and tsessebe.

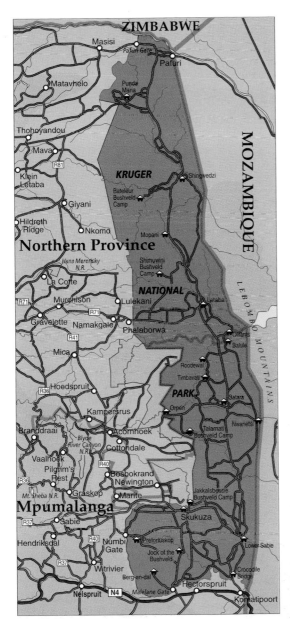

Opposite left: *Drought and searing heat dry up the already severely taxed water supplies in the Park with formerly perennial rivers being reduced to seasonal flows.*

Opposite bottom: *Forming the border with Mozambique, the scenic Lebombo Mountains form a charming backdrop for the flora-rich eastern region.*

Below: *The striking yellow-green fever tree (Acacia xanthophloea).*

SKUKUZA	J	F	M	A	M	J	J	A	S	O	N	D
MIN TEMP. °C	21	21	19	16	10	6	6	9	13	16	18	20
AV. MIN. TEMP. °F	70	70	66	61	50	43	43	48	55	61	64	68
AV. MAX. TEMP. °C	33	32	31	30	28	26	26	27	29	30	31	32
AV. MAX. TEMP. °F	91	90	88	86	82	79	79	81	84	86	88	90
RAINFALL mm.	93	87	73	33	14	10	10	6	26	35	76	84
RAINFALL in	4	3	3	1	0.3	0.5	0.5	0	1	1	3	3

Climate

Kruger has very hot, wet summers and cool, dry winters. Visiting the Park during the drier winter months (June – August) has the advantage that game-viewing is better. In winter, animals congregate in the vicinity of rivers or permanent waterholes and since the vegetation cover is reduced, viewing is made easier. The malaria risk is also minimal in winter. On the other hand, the wet summer does have other advantages. Trees and shrubs look splendid in their fresh foliage, flowers are plentiful and the atmosphere has a certain vibrance which the dry months of winter lack. Summer is also the time when most animals have their young. Many migrant birds also flock to the Park during the wet months.

Hottest days are experienced during November through to February when temperatures above 40°C (104°F) often occur. During those months the night-time temperatures drop to about 18°C (64°F). During winter, day-time temperatures from May through to July average a mild 26°C (78°F) but it gets cold at night, dropping to about 5°C (41°F). A distinct wet season exists, usually beginning in October and continuing through to April. But, even during this period, it is unusual to have more than four or five rainy days per month. Rain or overcast weather is highly unlikely during the months from May to August.

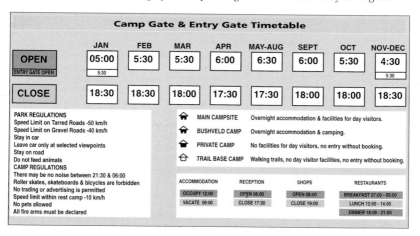

Camp Gate & Entry Gate Timetable

	JAN	FEB	MAR	APR	MAY-AUG	SEPT	OCT	NOV-DEC
OPEN (ENTRY GATE OPEN)	05:00 (5:30)	5:30	5:30	6:00	6:30	6:00	5:30	4:30 (5:30)
CLOSE	18:30	18:30	18:00	17:30	17:30	18:00	18:00	18:30

PARK REGULATIONS
Speed Limit on Tarred Roads -50 km/h
Speed Limit on Gravel Roads -40 km/h
Stay in car
Leave car only at selected viewpoints
Stay on road
Do not feed animals
CAMP REGULATIONS
There may be no noise between 21:30 & 06:00
Roller skates, skateboards & bicycles are forbidden
No trading or advertising is permitted
Speed limit within rest camp -10 km/h
No pets allowed
All fire arms must be declared

🏠 MAIN CAMPSITE — Overnight accommodation & facilities for day visitors.
🏠 BUSHVELD CAMP — Overnight accommodation & camping.
🏠 PRIVATE CAMP — No facilities for day visitors, no entry without booking.
⌂ TRAIL BASE CAMP — Walking trails, no day visitor facilities, no entry without booking.

ACCOMMODATION	RECEPTION	SHOPS	RESTAURANTS
OCCUPY 12:00	OPEN 08:00	OPEN 08:00	BREAKFAST 07:00 - 09:00
VACATE 09:00	CLOSE 17:30	CLOSE 19:00	LUNCH 12:00 - 14:00
			DINNER 18:00 - 21:00

Wildlife

So far, 147 species of mammals have been recorded in the Kruger National Park, the bulk (65%) being small species such as mice, shrews, bats, hares etc.

The Big Five: this is a term that was coined by hunters who risked life and limb in the far-flung corners of Africa. The 'Big Five' – elephant, rhino, buffalo, lion and leopard – describes those animals they considered the most dangerous. Rangers in Kruger, many of whom have had very narrow escapes, will confirm that the choice of animals is correct!

Most strongly evoking the image of untamed Africa, **lion** (*Panthera leo*) never fail to draw admiring gazes from even the most frequent visitor. Even in a restful, daytime mood, they have an air of dominance and raw power.

Although found throughout the Park, lion are more common south of the Olifants River, especially in the Central Plains around Satara, and also in the Tshokwane, Lower Sabie and Crocodile Bridge areas. Unlike other cats, lion are social and live in prides of usually one or two males, several females and their young offspring.

Exquisitely patterned, shy and secretive, **leopard** (*Panthera pardus*) are solitary cats found throughout the Park but are far more common in the riverine forest adjoining rivers such as the Sabie, Nwaswitsontso and Shingwedzi. They also like rocky outcrops and hills with

GIRAFFE

Giraffe reach up to 5.2m (17.16ft) in height and a bull may weigh between 970 to 1400kg (2100 – 3000lb). They can reach up to 30 years of age but are usually killed by lion much earlier. They are most often seen in herds of between two and six animals, feeding on leaves, especially those of *Acacia* trees. When fighting, bulls stand next to each other and use their heads as clubs for sideward blows.

IMPALA

Impala are by far the most abundant antelope species in Kruger, mostly seen in herds of between 10 to 60 individuals. They have a distinct mating season from April to June, when aggressive dominant rams separate from the bachelor herds to appropriate a harem of females. Males are commonly seen fighting during these months, one partner sometimes being mortally wounded in the sparring. Calves are born in late November or December.

Opposite: *Hot, dry terrain near the Engelhardt Dam.*
Left: *The regal male lion, largest of the world's cats and a pinnacle predator in the Kruger's diverse food chain.*

OXPECKERS
TOUGH ON TICKS

The common **red-billed oxpecker** and rare **yellow-billed oxpecker** are seen throughout Kruger, seated astride or scurrying along the sides, neck or even peeking into the ears of buffalo, giraffe and other animals. They are well-tolerated by their hosts, because they feed on ticks and other external parasites found on the skins of all wild animals. Each bird may eat as many as 1600 ticks per day.

Above: *Found predominantly in riverine forest, the exquisitely patterned leopard is a secretive creature, seldom viewed.*

patches of dense woodland. Leopard tend to rest by day, often in a tree, and become active at dusk. If you want to see leopard, your best chance would be to go on a river drive in the late afternoon or, better still, join one of the organized night drives.

With heavy sweeping horns present in both sexes, **buffalo** (*Syncerus caffer*) are widespread over the whole of Kruger, but are perhaps more easily seen in the open mopane-plains north of the Olifants River. Despite their size, and having a mass of up to 800kg (1750lb), buffalo are regularly caught by lion. A group of lion may circle a buffalo lagging behind a herd, then harass this animal for several hours, until finally a lion gets a good mouth-hold on the rump or hind-leg. The other lion then close in rapidly, avoiding the vicious swipes of the buffalo horns, until the injured animal drops and they can get a strangling neck-hold.

Black rhinoceros (*Diceros bicornis*) were heavily hunted in the 19th century and the scattered leftover individuals found it quite difficult to find mates. By 1946, the black rhino population of the Kruger had died out. In 1971 a reintroduction programme was initiated whereby 70 of these animals were brought in from KwaZulu-Natal and Zimbabwe. This population is now very slowly increasing in numbers.

Black rhino prefer densely wooded areas, and are most common south of the Sabie River, especially in the thickets between Lower Sabie and Crocodile Bridge.

They are solitary, the males maintaining discreet territories. Bulls can be very aggressive and often charge with minimal provocation.

Despite the name, **White rhinoceros** (*Ceratotherium simum*) are uniformly charcoal-grey in colour. No-one seems to be sure, but the name is thought to have come from 'wide'-lipped rhino (in contrast to the pointed lips of black rhino). They were exterminated in the Lowveld through excessive hunting, the last individuals disappearing late in the 19th century. In 1961 reintroductions were started from KwaZulu-Natal, the translocated animals doing so well that today nearly 2000 are living in Kruger.

The huge hulks of **elephant** (*Loxodonta africana*) are a familiar site in Kruger. They are more common in the northern half of the Park, but may be seen almost anywhere, although least frequently in the area between Berg-en-Dal and Pretoriuskop.

Elephant feed on an exceptionally wide range of leaves, grasses, bark, and will often also push over trees to reach the roots and fruit. They feed voraciously and take in about 250kg (550lb) of food every day.

Above: *Second largest of the Park's mammals, the powerful white rhino uses its flat lips to graze.*
Below: *Elephant gather at Shiloweni Dam. The adult African elephant will drink up to 120 litres of water and consume about 250kg (550lb) of food each day.*

Birdlife

If you are a bird-lover you will find Kruger something of a paradise! It has 484 different species, including many breathtakingly beautiful birds insistently vocalising in loud tones for all to hear. There are many species of **weaver** birds which construct elaborate nests, only to be rejected by a female demanding an even higher degree of perfection. In summer, huge squadrons of tiny seed-eating **queleas**, numbering hundreds of thousands, flock over the grassy plains of the Central District.

In summer **kingfishers** are common. You may see them hovering in their resplendent colours over a quiet pool, suddenly folding their wings to dive into the watery depths and emerge seconds later with a prize morsel. **Sunbirds**, **rollers**, **bee-eaters**, **orioles**, and numerous other dazzlingly brilliant birds will cause an involuntary remark of admiration each time they are seen.

There are also large birds, ranging from the extraordinary **secretary bird** and **ground hornbill**, to an array of stately **eagles**, up to the curious **ostrich** which quietly struts under the hot sun in the open veld. Various **ducks**, **storks** and numerous other birds will also be seen wherever you happen to base yourself in Kruger. The forest-fringes of the main rivers are the most rewarding for bird-watchers, and the Pafuri area in the Far North is renowned as being especially rich.

Right: *A magnificent solitary Martial eagle scans the area for hares, monkeys and squirrels, its primary prey.*

Plant Life

Plants are responsible for much of the atmosphere we experience in Kruger, while the distribution and density of all the animals is almost totally governed by them too. Plants provide food, shelter and habitat, and so are vitally important. Despite the relatively dry climate, Kruger is exceptionally rich in its variety of plants. About 1968 different species have been recorded, and are made up of 457 trees or shrubs, 235 grasses, 27 ferns, 16 woody lianas, 20 aloes and 1213 herbaceous plants.

In winter the veld usually appears harsh and arid, most of the trees having dropped their leaves and the grass a dreary yellow-brown. With the return of good rain, new growth surges from the ground, throwing out showers of bright foliage and flowers. Stop for a closer look at the aesthetic perfection of flowers such as the **flame lily** (*Gloriosa superba*), the **tumbleweeds** (*Boophane*) and **blood lilies** (*Scadoxus*), or the magnificent white or blue **water lilies** (*Nymphaea*).

Trees of magnificent stature and imposing form are numerous, and you'll certainly admire the statuesque shapes of long-dead **leadwood** trees (*Combretum imberbe*) which dot the savanna plains. Gigantic **Sycamore figs** (*Ficus sycomorus*) line all the rivers, and the impressive **baobabs** (*Adansonia digitata*) in the sun-drenched northern hills are also fascinating.

HOMEMADE JELLY AND WINE

Besides its attractive appearance, the **marula** tree (*Sclerocarya birrea*) produces large numbers of table-tennis sized fruit between December and February, avidly sought by elephant and many other animals. The fruit is also collected in many of Kruger's camps, from which a delicious jelly is prepared, either to spread on bread or to add to meat. Commercial ventures also sell **marula liqueur** which is very popular.

EUPHORBIA TREE

Resembling overgrown candelabra-like succulents, six species of *Euphorbia* trees occur in Kruger. They are most noticeable along the Lebombo Mountains, but specimens also grow in some camps such as Skukuza, Letaba and Olifants. When cut or otherwise injured, a milky latex seeps out which can harm the eyes or skin and can be extremely painful. Earlier inhabitants soaked dry grass with the latex and the grass was then tied around rocks and thrown into pools to kill fish.

Left: *The attractive marula tree has tasty fruit which is sought after by elephant and other animals. The fruit is also used to make a delicious marula liqueur.*

CULLING

The policy of killing a perceived excess of certain animals has given rise to (often heated) controversy ever since it was started in the mid-1960s. The basis of the policy is that, despite the large area of the Park, only certain areas are favoured by animals such as elephant and buffalo. When population numbers in those areas increase above a certain level, their numbers start to negatively influence other animals. This is most clearly seen around watering holes where the trampling effect of thousands of buffalo lays bare large areas. High elephant numbers also pose a threat to certain tree species, such as baobabs from which elephant love to strip bark.

Wildlife Conservation

Although Kruger's management policy is to keep human intervention to a minimum, the Park's ecosystem is no longer quite natural. For example, national veterinary laws require a fence around the Park, and when this was erected during the 1960s, animals could no longer follow ancient migratory routes to look for alternate sources of food and water during periods of scarcity. Fencing has also meant that when the density of elephant or buffalo becomes high, they no longer have their ancient freedom to filter off to less dense areas outside the Park. These animals are now restricted to Kruger, but their numbers cannot be allowed to increase indefinitely, so excess animals have to be removed either by moving them to other parks or by culling. There are many such examples, which collectively mean that – despite the enormous area of Kruger – the Park must still be managed, to some extent, like a game farm.

A team of full-time scientists is stationed in Kruger to research the various key facets of the ecosystem. Aside from their own projects, these researchers also collabo-

rate extensively with other scientists from universities around the world, making Kruger one of the most intensively researched national parks anywhere. The recommendations of these scientists are then submitted to Kruger's Standing Committee for Wildlife Management, after which approval is implemented by rangers and other field staff. Since it is Kruger's policy to ensure the well-being of all its species, population ceilings have been established for elephant, buffalo and hippo. Excess numbers are removed in the winter of each year either through capture and relocation to other conservation areas, or through culling when insufficient requests for live animals are received.

HISTORY IN BRIEF
Early Inhabitants

There is abundant evidence in the Kruger Park of an ancient and almost continuous presence of humans – albeit localized and at a low density – within the area. Implements which date back to the Stone Age were patiently chipped and shaped by the San. These cutting tools and other relics now lie dispossessed next to vantage-points overlooking dried-out pans at Pafuri, a silent testimony of human life long gone. The San hunter-gatherers also left a rich legacy of rock-paintings in caves and rock-overhangs, such as the one near the Hippo Pool near Crocodile Bridge.

Somewhere around the 2nd century AD the first of the Nguni-speaking people entered southern Africa. By about 400AD black people had settled along the Letaba River, splinter groups of a steady migration taking place from East Africa southwards along the east coast. This heralded the arrival of agriculturalists and herdsmen, who eventually displaced the San.

A New Way of Life

Artefacts and other evidence of early black settlements occur along most of the major rivers of the Park. Unlike the San who lived under rock overhangs, these new Iron Age migrants constructed huts of poles and mud with thatch roofs. Iron remnants are widespread throughout the Park: molten copper dated at 850AD has been found

Opposite: *Game capture and relocation to new parks is an important function of Kruger's staff.*
Above: *At Pafuri, Stone Age implements attest to the Park's early inhabitants.*

WINDOW INTO THE PAST

At **Thulamela** near Pafuri picnic site and **Masorini hill** near Phalaborwa gate, extensive evidence of previous human dwellings and activities exists. Archaeological studies have given a good insight into the daily lives of these early people, and reconstructions of village structures are now on display at these two places. A guide will take you around the area, giving you a fascinating tour back in time!

Above: *An Iron Age village at Masorini Hill in the Park's northern region.*

at a site near Balule and a piece of gold at Thulamela near Pafuri. They also kept cattle, sheep, goats, dogs, and cultivated beans and sorghum. Conditions for stock farming were not favourable, however, so that by about 800AD they relied on game for meat.

The small human population and their hunting techniques could not have had any significant impact on the wildlife or environment. Rather, their existence depended upon not depleting the local wildlife which they needed in order to survive.

KILLER VIRUS

Rinderpest swept through Africa during the 1890s, leaving a trail of death behind it, unprecedented in human history. It reached southern Africa in 1896, travelling south at an estimated 150km per week. Referred to as 'cattle plague' it decimated cattle and certain wildlife species, nearly wiping out the entire buffalo population of the Lowveld. It is thought the effects of this **epidemic** on the local human population were even more disastrous than the brutal Anglo-Boer War, a mere three years later.

Distant Arrivals

Elsewhere on the sub-continent, the first stirrings of far greater disruptive consequences were taking place. In 1652 the Dutch established a permanent colony at the Cape, and brought with them guns, ammunition, and horses. These early white settlers in the Cape found themselves amidst an astounding array of wildlife. They unfortunately hunted with great enthusiasm, soon eradicating elephant, hippo, lion and other animals which threatened their crops and livestock.

After the establishment of British rule at the Cape in 1806, rapidly escalating numbers of Boers (which is Afrikaans for 'Farmers') trekked north with ox-wagons in order to escape taxes imposed by the British authorities. In the 1850s they established the two independant Boer republics, the Orange Free State and the Transvaal.

Transvaal Lowveld

The main exploration of the Transvaal Lowveld took place during the early 19th century. These were efforts by the Boers who sought trading and transport routes to the coast of Portuguese East Africa (which is now Mozambique), wanting to avoid the ports of British-ruled Natal (which is now

KwaZulu-Natal). By the mid-19th century well-established wagon routes crossed the Lowveld to link Delagoa Bay (now Maputo Bay, in Mozambique) with Lydenburg and other settlements in the Transvaal republic. Way-stations and small settlements quickly sprang up.

The mopane-veld of the Eastern Transvaal was rich in elephant and ivory-hunting very soon flourished. Thousands of the animals were shot. In 1864 the annual shipment of just one merchant in the little hamlet of Schoemansdal amounted to an astonishing 16,000kg (35,280lbs) of ivory. This rich supply of game led to organized sprees of self-indulgent wildlife massacres.

Above: *A nostalgic painting of Boer (Afrikaner) trekkers struggling up a mountain pass with their heavily-laden ox-wagons. The Great Trek, as it has come to be known, was initiated in the 1830s and it gathered momentum as a mass exodus into the interior from the Cape. By 1850, two independant Boer republics had been created, namely the Transvaal and the Orange Free State.*

Left: *Aerial view of a gold mine near Gravelotte. Many areas near Kruger are rich in minerals and the discovery of gold in the 19th century opened the Lowveld region to a flood of prospectors from all over the world.*

BLOWING UP FISH

Dynamite was used extensively in the mining enterprises which sprang up in the Transvaal after the discovery of gold. Innovative fishermen soon learned that exploding dynamite in a river stunned large numbers of fish which soon floated to the surface. With an abundance of dynamite and ineffective regulations, fish were soon being blasted in large quantities in the Lowveld rivers. In 1880 legislation was introduced (Law no.5 of 1880) which made it a punishable offence to kill fish by the use of dynamite or other explosives.

Golden Times

The discovery of gold would change the Transvaal Lowveld forever, opening the region to a flood of people from all over the world. Adventurous prospectors found particularly rich deposits of the precious metal at Pilgrim's Rest in 1873 and Barberton in 1884. Towns were proclaimed, farms allocated and trade-links established. The people needed meat, and for diversion they also hunted for sport on a large scale.

Most of the pioneers settled along the escarpment. There was good reason for this. Malaria and other diseases such as horse-sickness were rife in the hot lowlands. Cattle were also decimated by tsetse-transmitted blood-parasites in the feared 'fly-belts'. While herds of game attracted numerous hunting parties temporarily into the area, no-one wished to settle in this inhospitable wilderness hugging the Lebombo Mountains and reaching all the way from the Crocodile River to the Limpopo River.

HISTORICAL CALENDAR

Pre-Christian era San Bushmen live in small groups in many areas of the current-day Kruger National Park, leaving abundant evidence through cave paintings.

400AD Black tribes people established along Letaba River, Mutlumuvi Spruit and several other sites. Rivalry caused them to eventually completely displace the San Bushmen.

Mid–19th century Small settlements of white *voortrekkers* are established mainly along the escarpment area, hunting parties entering the Lowveld for meat, skins and ivory.

1873 Gold discovered at Pilgrim's Rest. Large numbers of fortune seekers enter vicinity of the Eastern Transvaal Lowveld (known today as Mpumalanga).

1884 Gold discovered at Barberton. More people flood into the Lowveld, greatly increasing wildlife hunting.

1896 The continent-wide Rinderpest epidemic reaches southern Africa and decimates wildlife. Increased concern among the public over the severely depleted game stocks.

13 April 1898 Proclamation of the Sabi Government Reserve, an area between the Sabie and Crocodile rivers.

1899 Anglo-Boer War commences and culminates with the British winning the war. British rule begins in 1902.

July 1902 James Stevenson-Hamilton takes over as Warden of the Sabi Game Reserve, a fortuitous appointment as he would be a major force in wildlife conservation.

May 1903 The Singwitsi Game Reserve is proclaimed, a huge piece of land between the Letaba and Luvuvhu rivers.

31 May 1926 The Kruger National Park is proclaimed, incorporating the old Sabi and Singwitsi Game Reserves and the land in between.

1946 James Stevenson-Hamilton finally retires, having ensured that his 'Cinderella' had become a 'Princess'.

1995 Twenty-four camps with a total of 4000 beds available in Kruger. Some 600,000 visitors now enter the Park every year.

Left: *Owing to effective management, wildlife populations have regained much of their former glory.*

Voices of Concern

The dwindling herds of game did not go unnoticed, but laws and regulations did little to stifle the deeply instilled hunting ethic. Yet another calamity struck: the Rinderpest virus reached southern Africa in 1896, leaving bloating carcasses over the entire subcontinent.

Buffalo, warthog and many other animals were reduced to shockingly low numbers. Although the idea of a game reserve had already been discussed on several occasions by the Volksraad (Peoples' council) of the Republic, it was only in 1898 that a majority of the legislature would vote in favour, and on 13 April of that year the momentous proclamation of a Government Reserve appeared in the *Staatscourant* (State gazette). It comprised of a stretch of land between the Sabie and Crocodile rivers, small in comparison with the current-day Kruger National Park, but an important first step in preserving the country's wildlife heritage.

A Faltering Start

In 1899 the Anglo-Boer War began, and British rule was imposed in 1902. Even before the end of the war, the British had secured control of the Eastern Transvaal (now known as Mpumalanga) and stationed civil servants in strategic positions. In 1901 a Captain HF Francis was appointed Game Inspector of the Sabi Game Reserve and, later, a previous mineral prospector, WM Walker, was appointed as Warden. But Walker was ineffective and he was dismissed in January 1902.

FEVER

The early pioneers had no idea that mosquitoes transmitted **malaria**, or what caused the disease. Yet it was probably the most common affliction in the Lowveld and wreaked havoc during the wet summer months. Starting in 1887, construction of the railway line from Lourenço Marques (now Maputo) through the Crocodile River valley immediately south of the present Kruger Park was accompanied by great loss of human life. TV Bulpin, in his book *Lost Trails of the Transvaal*, says that 'On the average, 135 men in every 1000 died of fever all along the line, and every individual suffered from it to some degree'. In the nine-month period required to build the line from Lourenzo Marques to the South African border, more than 200 men unfortunately died of malaria, many of them contract workers from the Netherlands.

Right: James Stevenson-Hamilton, visionary and conservationist, was instrumental in establishing the present Kruger Park.

Bolder Beginnings

In July 1902 Major James Stevenson-Hamilton entered the Sabi Game Reserve to take office as Warden. He based himself at Sabi Bridge (now Skukuza) and immediately installed proper administrative procedures. He also set about making sure he had enough powers to perform his job, soon being appointed Resident Justice of the Peace and Native Commissioner with full police powers and authority to stop activities relating to mining and prospecting in his area of jurisdiction.

Not an idle person, he had inspected the region on horseback within two months, making recommendations that the Reserve should be extended to the Olifants River and westwards to the watershed (escarpment). This new section comprised both State land and private, unused farms. He negotiated agreements with landowners over game protection rights and in August 1903 the entire extension was gazetted as protected land. Furthermore, in May 1903, the government also proclaimed the Singwitsi Game Reserve, a huge tract adjoining the Lebombo Mountains between the Letaba and Pafuri (Luvuvhu) rivers.

JAMES STEVENSON-HAMILTON

If any one person can be singled out as being most instrumental in helping to establish the Kruger National Park, it would without doubt be Colonel James Stevenson-Hamilton. Born in 1867 in Scotland into an affluent family, he opted for a military life, becoming an officer in the Inniskilling Dragoons. During military service he developed a deep affinity for Africa, and after serving in the Anglo-Boer War he accepted the post as Warden of the Sabi Game Reserve. He was to stay on in that position for the next 44 years, finally retiring in 1946. He had superb attributes of high intelligence, discipline, debating and negotiating skills, tenacity, and also physical toughness. Gratitude is due to this incredible man for his firmness of conviction and unfailing efforts to bring about one of the finest national parks in the world.

Setting to Work

Stevenson-Hamilton's strategy was to divide the entire area into administrative blocks, appointing in each block a Ranger with a handful of assistants. He was a strict disciplinarian and even officialdom soon learnt that no exceptions or privileges were granted. He successfully prosecuted two senior police officials for poaching, bringing great hostility against him.

To build up the decimated herds of game, he began reducing predator numbers; lion, leopard, wild dog and other carnivores were shot on sight.

Uneasy Times

But far greater problems lay ahead. Although his views on game protection and the proclamation of reserves were actively supported by the Commissioner of Native Affairs, Sir Godfrey Lagden, several other government bodies were against the reserves. The departments of Mines, Lands, and Agriculture wanted this land to be economically exploited, and powerful lobbies representing landowners and other interest groups also voiced their resentment. Stevenson-Hamilton tirelessly advanced the idea of a 'National Park' where visitors could view wildlife for relaxation and enjoyment. After a period of particularly strong opposition between 1910 and 1923, the National Park concept gained momentum and became widely accepted. Finally, on 31 May 1926, Piet Grobler, the Minister of Lands, proclaimed the proposed area as the Kruger National Park. It included the old Sabi and Singwitsi Game Reserves as well as the land in between.

ASHES TO ASHES

James Stevenson-Hamilton became Warden of the Sabi Game Reserve – later to be expanded as the Kruger National Park – in 1902. During his 44 years of service his efficiency and impact was of a standard comparable to the best nature conservators anywhere in the world. He died on 10 December 1957. His ashes have been scattered over a massive granite outcrop near Skukuza. There is a memorial plaque at the popular look-out point on this hill.

Left: *Warthogs pay homage to the founding father of their present sanctuary.*

Fresh Challenges

James Stevenson-Hamilton and his staff began to pour all their energies into the construction of roads and camps in and around the Kruger National Park. By 1928, 196km (122 miles) of road had been completed, and by 1936 this had climbed to 1450 km (900 miles). Summer rain would transform these roads into muddy quagmires, and flooded rivers would isolate one from outside assistance for several days. Yet tourist numbers actually began to increase, the wilderness atmosphere drawing more and more enthusiasts. From the hesitant beginnings of three cars entering in 1927, yielding a total income of R15 for that year, the figure later blossomed to 6000 cars carrying 26,000 people in 1935.

By the mid-1990s a sophisticated organization had evolved, a leader in its field providing assistance throughout Africa. From meagre beginnings a century ago, the Kruger National Park had come a long way.

CAMP VIEWING	GAME	ATMOSPHERE	SCENERY	RIVER/DAM	RATING
Balule	Good	Average	Good	Not in sight	Infrastructure very poor
Berg-en-Dal	Poor	Average	Average	Stream/Dam	Low
Crocodile Bridge	Good	Average	Average	Not in Sight	Low
Letaba	Good	Good	Good	River	Very High
Lower Sabie	Good	Good	Good	River/Dam	Very High
Mopani	Average	Average	Average	Dam	Low
Olifants	Good	Average	Good	River	Moderate
Orpen	Good	Average	Average	None	Low
Pretoriuskop	Average	Average	Average	None	Low
Punda Maria	Good	Average	Average	None	Moderate
Satara	Good	Good	Good	None	Very High
Shingwedzi	Good	Good	Good	River	High
Skukuza	Good	Average	Good	River	High

THE CAMPS

There are 24 camps in the Kruger National Park. Don't camp alone or 'rough it' in the bush by yourself. Rangers are concerned that you are either going to poach or be eaten by lion! With the exception of only a few

camps which have deliberately been left fairly primitive and rustic for die-hard enthusiasts, all other camps offer a surprising range of accommodation, from luxury houses to furnished tents (yes, even the tents have electric lights!), or stands where you can put up your own tent or camper-van. There are three categories of camps, each differing in the basic facilities.

Main camps are by-and-large the largest of the lot, and provide the bulk of the almost 4000 beds on offer each night in Kruger. They contain a selection of Donor houses, luxury cottages, chalets or huts and usually also a camping area. Depending on your budget or whim, you may choose to dine at a restaurant offering multiple-course meals, perhaps opt for a lighter meal at a fast-food cafeteria, or buy your own ingredients and other necessities in the well-stocked shops for preparation in your own kitchenette. You will find enough conveniences and amenities in these camps to make your stay comfortable, including air-conditioning and refrigerators as standard fittings in most accommodation units. All main camps have fuel stations, a few offer vehicle repair services, some even have a swimming pool. Virtually all are set in scenic surrounds, with spacious, meticulously-kept lawns and large trees providing welcome shade between the bungalows.

Above: *A lion crossing the road causes a temporary traffic jam as windows unwind and cameras begin clicking.*
Below: *Caravanning and tenting are popular tourist pursuits, with facilities available at many camps.*

Bushveld Camps	Game Viewing	Atmosphere	Scenery	River/Dam	Rating
Bateleur	Poor	Good	Average	Dry river	Moderate
Biyamiti	Good	Good	Good	Seasonal river	High
Jakkalsbessie	Good	Average	Good	River	High
Shimuwini	Average	Good	Average	Dam	High
Sirheni	Good	Good	Average	Dam	High
Talamati	Good	Good	Average	Dry river	High

The facilities in the Main camps are available to anyone visiting Kruger, unlike the following camps which are only accessible to visitors actually staying overnight. **Bushveld camps** are smaller, most having about 15 cottages which can be rented individually (unlike Private camps where the entire camp has to be reserved and occupied by one group). Bushveld camps have great atmosphere, privacy, peace and quiet, but you will have to do your own cooking. No restaurants are available, neither is a shop or fuel station. You must buy all your supplies beforehand from the nearest Main camp which is always within an hour's drive. That does not mean the camps are primitive! The cottages are all very comfortable, and you can choose between three-bedroomed, two- or one-bedroomed units. All have kitchenettes and refrigerators. The access roads to these camps are off-limits to non-residents, so you are guaranteed privacy. No camping is allowed.

Private camps accommodate between 12 and 18 people, and you have to reserve the entire camp; you pay the full fee whether you use only half the available facilities or all. Getting a group of friends to share the fee makes it affordable, and you will have the camp all to yourselves! Cottages are comfortable with all the necessary facilities, but you have to shop and refuel at the nearest Main camp. Access roads to these camps are also private, so you temporarily own your own corner of paradise.

Private Camps	Game Viewing	Atmosphere	Scenery	River/Dam	Rating
Boulders	Poor	Average	Average	None	Low
Jock of the Bushveld	Good	Good	Good	Dry river	High
Malelane	Average	Average	Average	Not in view	Low
Nwanetsi	Good	Good	Good	Not in view	High
Roodewal	Good	Good	Good	Dry river	High

CARAVANS AND CAMPING

Camping space for **tents** or **caravans** is available in Balule, Berg-en-Dal, Crocodile Bridge, Letaba, Marula, Lower Sabie, Pretoriuskop, Punda Maria, Satara, Shingwedzi and Skukuza. Except for a few sites at Skukuza, **no electrical outlets** are available for camping sites and Park rules stipulate that you may run a portable power generator only 'from one hour after sunrise to one hour before sunset' to minimise disturbing the other visitors. Good communal kitchen and ablution facilities have also been laid on for campers.

Accommodation

Kruger tends to cater more for mid-range budgets, and within that cost-bracket the various options available are plentiful! Real **bottom-of-the-barrel** budgeters may find their choice somewhat limited, but don't despair too much – some camps have cheaper bungalows, many camps have furnished tents and, if you split costs with a companion, it may well suit your pocket.

Campsites where you may pitch your tent or park a caravan are available in all the Main camps. Excellent ablution and basic cooking facilities are available in all the camping grounds. You either bring your own tent, or hire one of the ready-pitched, fully-furnished ones.

If you find all the options a bit confusing, keep the following factors in mind. How many people are in your group, and would you prefer everyone to be together, as in a **donor House**, or don't you mind being separate, as in **family cottages** or **huts**? Are you going to need cooking facilities, such as a **chalet with kitchen**, or eat in the restaurant or cafeteria? In this case you would require a **chalet without a kitchen**. If a good view is important, then ask for a riverside hut.

Above: *Olifants Camp is wonderfully situated above the attractive Olifants River.*
Below: *Family chalets with or without kitchens are examples of the variety of accommodation available in the Park.*

ACCOMMODATION AND TRAVEL

There are 24 camps in Kruger, varying in size and well spread over the territory, often in a magnificent setting overlooking rivers or luxuriant scenery. Altogether these camps offer almost 4000 beds on any given night, ranging from no-frills two-bedded huts, various mid-range options, to luxury multi-roomed cottages. A network of roads consisting of 882km (550 miles) of tarred surface and an additional 1703km (1060 miles) of gravel road – all of a high standard – give you access to all parts of the Park.

Basic choices are between **donor houses** which are present in all the Main camps, accommodate up to eight people, and have a spacious kitchen, lounge area and verandah; **cottages** which vary from single to three-bedroomed, accommodate up to six people, have small kitchens and one or two bathrooms; a mix of single or double-bedroomed **chalets**, **rondavels**, or **huts** with or without private bathrooms and accommodating up to four people, and the **furnished tents** in the camping areas which have two beds and are surprisingly comfortable with table, chairs and electricity.

General Facilities

Should you forget anything in the last-minute rush before heading out for Kruger, you will be able to make do provided you remember that most important commodity – money! Each of the major camps has a **shop** where you can buy food; drinks ranging from bottled mineral water to strong alcohol; books; basic medicines; and curios. The Skukuza shop even has a **one-hour photo-print kiosk**. Curios are expensive, but then that is true for all South African curio shops. Most camps have a **licensed restaurant**, and even some of the Picnic Sites serve a variety of snacks and other refreshments. Each accommodation unit, including a camping stand, has a **barbecue facility**, using wood or charcoal which you can buy at the shop. There are also barbecue areas for day visitors in most camps and all

Right: *Good restaurants are situated in all the main camps. Here, the pleasant verandah at Berg-en-Dal is perfect for an afternoon drink before venturing into the hot African sun.*

picnic sites, with gas-fired grills. **Fuel** is sold in all the Main Camps, while the **Automobile Association** has emergency **vehicle repair facilities** in Skukuza, Satara and Letaba. Skukuza is the only camp which has a **bank** (Volkskas), with an **automated teller** accepting cards of all the

other major banks. Money is always welcome, so there is no problem paying with your **credit card** or by **cheque** anywhere in Kruger. All the camps have **telephones**, most using phonecards which are usually sold in the camp Reception Office. Skukuza has a **Post Office**. There are **doctors consulting rooms** in Skukuza where most emergency treatments can be done, and they have a well-stocked pharmacy. **Car-hire** (Avis) can be done in Skukuza (they will deliver to other camps), and there is an **airport** 4km (2½ miles) outside Skukuza with **daily Comair flights** to-and-from the Johannesburg International Airport. Finally, for that dirty laundry you don't feel like washing, many of the larger camps have coin-operated **launderettes** and **tumble driers** in the camping area among the tents and caravans.

Above: *Barbecue facilities are popular in most of the camps and picnic sites, making them ideal places to stop for lunch.*
Below: *For a well-deserved rest during a day's game-viewing, some pretty picnic spots like this one at Tshokwane serve refreshments and snacks.*

KEYS AND LOCKS

Kruger is a surreal island of peace and harmony in our world of violence and crime. You might be disconcerted at first to realize that no keys are provided to accommodation units, nor are there any lock-up facilities elsewhere. Theft is very much the exception, but for your own peace of mind try to keep your valuables close at hand or locked in a vehicle.

FUN ACTIVITIES

The **Elephant Hall** in Letaba and the **Stevenson-Hamilton Memorial Library** in Skukuza are well worth a visit. The spacious Elephant Hall has original skulls and tusks of some of the biggest elephants which have roamed Africa, including the so-called 'Magnificent Seven'. There are also a number of other interesting displays related to elephant. The Stevenson-Hamilton Library is an interesting, imposing structure, and also houses a collection of rare Africana and some interesting displays, such as that of the lion attack on Ranger Harry Wolhuter.

Below: *A midday dip is just the thing to prepare one for further game-viewing in the hot summer months.*

Recreation

Kruger's main attraction, of course, is game viewing, but there are leisure hours back in camp. You are not going to find play-parks, mini-zoos, or even television in the camps. Entertainment in Kruger is low-key which is a deliberate attempt to retain the wilderness atmosphere.

Favourites with the children in the hot summers are **swimming pools** which are large, well-maintained and have crystal clear water. You'll find pools in Pretoriuskop, Berg-en-Dal, Shingwedzi and Punda Maria. Many camps have **open-air** or **enclosed displays** relating to wildlife – don't miss the Elephant Hall in Letaba if you're in the vicinity and the Stevenson-Hamilton Memorial Library in Skukuza (despite its name it also has many interesting wildlife displays). Some have **walks** within the camp taking in historic sites, unusual trees, pleasant scenery, or rich birding areas; Berg-en-Dal even has a 'Braille walk' with a rope as a guide! As a change, you might opt to go on one of the day or night **guided game drives**, exposing you either to roads you wouldn't normally have access to, or night animals such as civet cat, genet, or other animals which are common at night but very rarely seen by day .

At night – if you're not on the night drive – you can dine in the **restaurant** where you will be served in old-world style. Each meal, by the way, is announced by the

Left: *Excellent, informative wildlife films can be viewed at night in the open-air amphitheatres at most of the larger camps.*

deep beat of **African drums** which is a fascinating minor ritual to behold. Don't expect sophisticated cuisine – it's usually a basic course of soup, fish, venison with vegetables, followed by a sweet, tea or coffee, cheese and biscuits. Most of the larger camps have open-air amphitheatres where at night **wildlife films** are screened. These films have been produced mostly by world-class film-makers who have been converging on Kruger in recent years.

Wilderness Trails

Of all the wilderness experiences offered in Kruger, this is the closest you will get to reverting to primeval roots – in comfort and without having to put on your loincloths! Wilderness trails last two days and three nights, sleeping in rustic thatch-roofed huts and walking around in the most remote and undisturbed areas of the Park where no other visitors come. You can admire the many San paintings which adorn the caves and overhangs in the hills, clamber over the bouldered Lebombo Mountains to scan untouched wilderness as far as the eye can see, or absorb the atmosphere of the lush forest adjoining the Luvuvhu River. You will be part of a group of eight traillists, with two rangers who will look after you and with whom you are likely to establish a bond. It is an experience you are almost guaranteed never to forget.

NIGHT DRIVES

Driving around the Park at night in an open-sided vehicle with a Parks Board guide adds a whole new experience to your trip. Some would say it's expensive, but it's the only way you're going to get out at night, and as a once-off treat to yourself it's worth the cost. Ask the Reception Office about these (and the **day drives** if you like). The usual cost is R50 per adult, half price for children 6–12 yrs old (but these costs may change from time to time). No children under six are allowed. Your name will be put on a list, and half an hour before gate-closing time you will pile into a truck, and then ride off into the sunset armed with a spotlight. Bring your own snacks and something warm to wear. The trip lasts from three to four hours, and you should see hyena, genet, civet cat, often lion and leopard, aside from the more usual impala and kudu.

TRAIL RANGERS

Your trail ranger might look young, but he has undergone lots of training. He has also been through a rigorous selection process, and to test his 'cool' and reaction under duress he has had to demonstrate his skills in some rather harrowing circumstances. Trust him and listen to him. Feel reassured by the fact that several of them have had to actually shoot rhino and buffalo at close range during the course of some never-to-be-forgotten trails but they've always brought their charges back home safely.

Below: *A trail ranger leads guests out of the base camp on one of the Park's many exciting wilderness trails.*

Your trail ranger will meet up with you at the designated main camp mid-afternoon on Sunday or Wednesday. You will travel in a four-wheel-drive truck to your Wilderness Base-camp, in time for a sundowner drink and a familiarizing chat around the fire. Don't expect caviar and Chivaz Regal. Food is basic but you certainly won't starve. Take along some alcoholic drinks and small luxuries if you feel like it. Each hut has two bunks, and you will likely be lulled to sleep by the distant (sometimes alarmingly close!) calls of nightjars, hyena, lion or jackal. After early-morning coffee you will go on your first walk. A hushed excitement is always present in the crisp morning freshness. Your ranger will probably stop regularly to explain the details of a fascinating range of natural wonders. Along the way, at a particularly scenic or interesting spot, you'll stop for a light breakfast (cheese, fruit, nuts, biscuits, fruit juice), returning at about 11:00 for a welcome break before lunch. Then a siesta until about 15:00, refreshments and then hop aboard the truck for a bushveld drive to a different but equally interesting area for another walk. Finally you'll head back to camp for dinner (barbecue or stew, with vegetables and salads). The same basic routine will be followed the next day – but in the other areas of your vast wilderness region. All too soon the third morning dawns and you have to pack up and return to civilization thoroughly refreshed but greatly disappointed that the trip is over.

There are five Wilderness Trails in
Kruger, all set in their own large slice
of wild Africa, with no tourist camps,
traffic, or contact with other humans.
The **Bushman Trail** near Berg-en-Dal
is excellent for viewing San paintings,
seeing rhino and a range of other
animals, and exploring the great hill-
country which makes for wonderful
exploratory walks. The **Wolhuter Trail**
between Berg-en-Dal and Skukuza and
the **Napi Trail** near Pretoriuskop are
both good for spotting rhino and lion
and present a good opportunity to see

an impressive mix of other game. The **Metsi-Metsi Trail**
near Tshokwane is excellent for lion, leopard, buffalo,
giraffe and lots of other game, while the **Sweni Trail**
near Satara is very popular for all-round game-viewing,
scenery and atmosphere. The **Olifants Trail** near Olifants
camp is set in mountainous terrain, overlooks the Olifants
River and has great scenery with an excellent chance of
seeing a wide range of animals. Finally, adjoining the
Luvuvhu River north of Punda Maria, the **Nyalaland
Trail**, offers exceptional scenery, but don't expect to see
much game. This trail is the best for birding but tell your
ranger you're keen to see birds so he can concentrate on
finding the rare ones for you – including Pel's Fishing
Owl, Narina Trogon, crested guineafowl, and others!

Above: *A nervous kudu
cow, alert and attentive.*
Below: *Guinea fowl and
impala are common sights on
the wilderness trail routes.*

WHAT TO TAKE ON TRAIL

A hat, light clothes, light can-
vas or other walking shoes
(heavy leather boots provide
more discomfort than practi-
cal value), some mosquito
repellant, a flashlight (torch),
personal toiletries, a book,
camera, and binoculars if you
like. If you are going to need
alcoholic sustenance, take
that along as well. Everything
else is provided (including
backpacks and waterbottles).

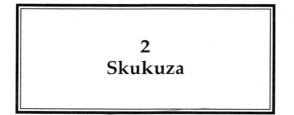

2
Skukuza

In Kruger, 'all roads lead to Skukuza'. It is the Park's headquarters and by far the largest camp, offering conveniences and facilities (bank, post office, airport etc.) not available elsewhere. Because it is close to a major entrance gate (Kruger Gate) and has an airport nearby, it is a convenient staging base or starting point for your holiday in the Park, and in fact a lot of people prefer staying here for their entire holiday. It is particularly convenient if you only have a weekend at your disposal, in which case you can fly down to Skukuza, hire a car, and enjoy the excellent drives and scenery around this famous camp. Game-viewing is good. You'll see a wide variety of game, and bird-watching along the Sabie River is excellent. This chapter will give you some idea of what to expect; what you can do; as well as a few game drives which you might also try.

THE SCENERY

Like much of the entire southern part of Kruger, the area around Skukuza is densely vegetated, dominated by knobthorn *Acacia* trees and *Combretum* bushwillow. Many other species such as marula and leadwood trees add atmosphere to the bush. Most of the country is flat, although occasional granite-bouldered hills are sprinkled over the landscape.

The Sabie River flows through the area, fringed by a rich complement of towering Sycamore figs and other trees, plus the associated birdlife and habitat for hippo, leopard and even elusive nyala.

DON'T MISS

*** **Sabie River drive:** the famous 'lion route' with lush riverside vegetation and abundant wildlife.
*** **Tshokwane picnic spot:** Kruger's top stopover where you will find numerous birds under shady trees.
** **Stevenson Hamilton Memorial Centre:** in Skukuza; many wildlife displays, historical artefacts, magazines etc.
** **Bird-hide:** outside Skukuza; mesmerizing view of dam and bird-watching in comfort.

Opposite: *Despite its size, Skukuza still retains much of its wilderness allure.*

Above: *An excellent way to enter the Park is through Skukuza's airport, with daily scheduled flights to and from Johannesburg.*

You are sure to see plenty of **impala** in this area, their sleek and graceful fawn-coloured forms being one of the memories you will carry home with you. This is also a good area for seeing kudu, duiker, steenbok, bushbuck and the lanky giraffe. Spend enough time driving around and you'll be unlucky if you don't come across lion, wild dog, rhino and elephant which are fairly common here. Slightly less common, but still regularly seen, are leopard and cheetah, a sighting which will be sure to give you an adrenalin rush!

PENDULOUS PODS

Seen along the Sabie River and also in Skukuza camp are the attractive and often very large **sausage trees** *(Kigelia africana)*. Sometime between July and October they sprout large, trumpet-shaped red flowers which open at night and last one or two days. From these develop the characteristic 'sausage' pods for which these trees are so well known. Heavy, thick and up to half a metre long (1.6ft), the fibrous pods are chewed by baboons but shunned by other animals. The pods usually drop around March/April, and it is a good idea not to loiter too long under one of these trees at such a time!

SKUKUZA

Skukuza is the place where most tourists head to for their first experience of a national park in Africa. It is one of the easiest parks to get to as the airport is so close by. It is the administrative headquarters of Kruger with a large staff complement, capable of accommodating well over 500 visitors. The camp lies sprawled on the southern bank of the Sabie River, with numerous shade-providing trees which have been planted over the years. Tidy green lawns are inviting and the perfect place to spread a blanket or for children to play games. The camp is geared towards providing you with a comfortable stay! There is a large camping area, well serviced with the usual cooking and ablution facilities, as well as a coin-operated launderette.

If you are unlucky and develop car trouble unexpectedly, the **Automobile Association** has an **Emergency Repair** branch in Skukuza, with tow-in facilities. Near the camp's main entrance is an attractive **Reception Office/Volkskas Bank/Post Office** complex. This is usually your first port of call when booked into Skukuza and also the meeting place when going on a **night drive.**

There are some attractive bronze impala figures next to the fishpond in front of the post office, a popular backdrop for family pictures! Nearby, against a wall, are bronze facemounts of the 'Founding Fathers' – Paul Kruger, James Stevenson-Hamilton and Piet Grobler, with a plaque giving some information. If you really feel the urge to re-establish links with the outside world, the post office has several public **telephones** outside, some coin-operated while others use phonecards which you can buy in the post office. And then, handy for late-comers after an extended game-viewing drive, there is an **automated teller** outside Volkskas bank which accepts cards of all the other major South African banks. Finally, for those unforeseen emergencies or aching backs, two **medical doctors** with a good range of diagnostic and treatment facilities, as well as a reasonably well-stocked pharmacy, have a clinic right inside the camp.

> ### A NEW BROOM
>
> **Sikhukhuza** and not Skukuza was the Zulu name given to Colonel James Stevenson-Hamilton, Warden of the Sabi Game Reserve from 1902. It means 'he who sweeps clean or levels the ground', apparently in reference to the sweeping new rules he imposed in his campaign against poaching.

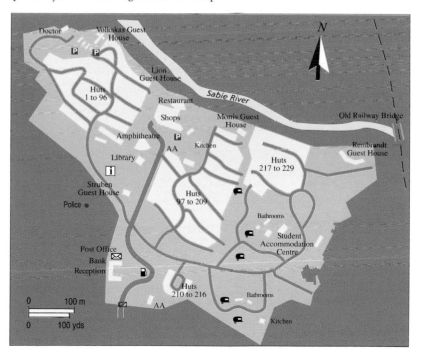

Above: *The Skukuza shop will satisfy all your everyday needs and has a great collection of curios.*

The Skukuza shop is enormous compared with shops you would normally find in African parks and it is well stocked with foodstuffs, medicines, film, curios and even a wide selection of clothes, books and magazines.

Skukuza also has an enormous licenced **restaurant** with some magnificent wooden furniture. The food is served buffet style and is usually good. Adjoining the restaurant is a spacious cafeteria serving a range of hamburgers and other fast food. The camp also has a little bakery which produces fresh bread, buns and other goodies. Previously a major attraction, the à la carte **Selati Train Restaurant** burnt down in early 1995 but there is talk of replacing it with a '**bushveld boma**' (open fire with rustic atmosphere but good food) and it should be in place at the time of going to press.

LITTLE HEROES ACRE

Dogs are indispensable colleagues of rangers, often being the only means of tracking a wounded leopard in dense bush, or distracting a charging lion for the few crucial seconds while a ranger unshoulders his rifle. Near the Stevenson-Hamilton Library, a small area has been set aside to house the gravestones of some of these staunch compatriots. It's a short stroll from the shop, just above the parking area for buses, next to the Library. Combine it with a visit to the static displays (rhino skeletons etc.) within view nearby.

Highlights of Skukuza

Skukuza itself has a number of attractions which you can visit, the first being the **Stevenson-Hamilton Memorial Library**. It's not just a library. They also have some interesting displays relating to wildlife and the early history of the Park. For example, the knife used by **Harry Wolhuter** in his much-related struggle with a lion is on display, together with a lion skin and a brief description of the whole incident. The stone-and-thatch building itself

is very attractive and has some absolutely magnificent fig trees outside, with their enormous branches spreading out to welcome you into their shade. Just below the Stevenson-Hamilton Library is an open-air amphitheatre where **wildlife films** are screened on most nights (except Sunday), and are usually of good quality.

If you feel like treating yourself and your partner, book seats at the **Bushveld Boma** which serves excellent food in good surroundings (enquire about this at the camp Reception Office). Other highlights are the day drives and night drives accompanied by Park guides, offering opportunities for game-viewing not usually available to visitors. Enquire about these at the Reception Office. A great way to spend a quiet hour is to drive the route to the **Skukuza Plant Nursery** (the turnoff is on the Kruger Gate road). Along the way you will find the bird-hide overlooking a dam, usually with some herons, darters, kingfishers, ducks or other waterbirds to keep you alert. There is ample parking. From here you walk along a reed-fenced 'safety-passage' which leads you into the attractive wood-frame hide, elevated slightly above water-level. Although at least 20 people could sit there, it is rare to find more than five at any time. The atmosphere is very relaxing and it's worth the few kilometres drive.

Opposite below:
Skukuza's enormous restaurant and cafeteria.
Above: *All aboard for an exciting night drive, booked at the Skukuza reception.*
Below: *Walking the safety passage to the bird-hide overlooking a dam.*

Above: *Lionesses pad along the famous 'lion route' road on the Sabie River drive. The region near the river is thickly vegetated and richly abundant in wildlife.*

BEST DRIVES
Skukuza to Lower Sabie ★★★

Famed as **The Lion Drive**, the H4-1 route which closely parallels the Sabie River between Skukuza and Lower Sabie is among the top five game-viewing roads available anywhere in Kruger National Park. Not only does it have an excellent selection of game which will surprise you at regular intervals but the birdlife is rich and the scenery is great. Add to that the frequent stretches of road which allow for magnificent panoramic views of the sparkling river below and you have a combination which is difficult to beat! The main road is tarred for its entire length but there are numerous side-roads turning off to allow closer access to the river and although these are gravel-surfaced they are maintained in perfect condition to ensure a comfortable drive.

The initial stretch between Skukuza and Nkuhlu Picnic Spot is rather densely covered with a mixture of sicklebush, acacias, tambotie and many other trees while the river edge is packed with a lush and highly attractive fringe of evergreen mahoganies, jackalberries, gigantic figs and statuesquely contorted apple-leaf trees. Vervet monkeys and baboons are plentiful here and have become rather tame and so will occasionally jump onto your car. From these vantage points, they frown and peer expectantly through the window in the hope of being given some leftover scraps. Don't succumb to the temptation to feed them! Also plentiful are warthogs, impala and kudu and you are bound to come across some hippo lazing in the placid water of the river along one of the gravel turnoffs. At some of these stops, flat rocks or sandbeds jut into the river and are favoured basking sites for crocodiles.

Conveniently halfway along your journey to Lower Sabie you reach the highly popular **Nkuhlu Picnic Spot**. By now you will probably feel like stretching your legs, going to the toilet and relaxing for a while in the peaceful atmosphere of the many mahogany trees and the river flowing silently by. There are many amenities here, including a kiosk which serves tea or coffee and other refreshments. If you're in the mood to barbecue there is a good supply of gas or wood-fired barbecues here which is a wonderful place to spend an hour or two out in the open. Good photographic opportunities often present themselves with the monkeys and numerous birds which gambol about the trees.

The stretch between Nkuhlu Picnic Spot and Lower Sabie is particularly good for elephant, lion, buffalo and, if you're lucky, also leopard. With so many trees present, birds are numerous and diverse. Yellow-billed hornbills are a perennial favourite among photographers but there are also bull-bulls, barbets, francolins, guineafowl, exquisitely coloured bee-eaters and much, much more. About 23km (14 miles) from Nkuhlu, very close to Lower Sabie, you reach **Sunset Dam**. Not a very original name but appropriate since so many residents of Lower Sabie camp spend the last waning moments of daylight here before returning to camp which is only two minutes drive away. It's a very scenic spot with hippo, crocodiles and plenty of waterbirds always in view. Photographers love this place because the chances of getting close-up shots of kingfishers, darters or storks are excellent.

ROUTE MARKERS

All roads in Kruger have **code numbers**, and using these codes will avoid confusion about which road is being referred to. The tarred trunk routes start with an H, such as the H4-1 linking Skukuza and Lower Sabie, while secondary roads start with an **S**, such as the **S25** between Crocodile Bridge and Malelane. Secondary roads are not tarred, but they are maintained in excellent condition and you need not be concerned about damage to your car. You may, however, need to rinse off the inevitable coat of dust!

Below: *The popular Nkuhlu Picnic Spot has many convenient amenities and is pleasantly situated along the Sabie River.*

Above: *Smoothly eroded boulders and attractive reed clumps make ideal photographic opportunities alongside the Sabie River.*

BABOONS

Never found far from permanent water, baboons usually occur in troops of about 10 to 30. They have a definite social hierarchy or 'pecking order', with a dominant male in charge and several large 'toughs' as his commandants. Their often human-like behaviour may be appealing and the playful youngsters irresistibly cuddly, **but baboons can be dangerous! Never feed baboons**, for good reasons. Soon they expect to be fed, and become quite aggressive if not given something. Some visitors have been badly frightened by baboons which were climbing into cars to help themselves to fruit or other food left in open view.

Skukuza to Tshokwane ***

This route takes you through classic Bushveld Africa with abundant game intermittently filling the wide expanses of breathtaking grass-covered savannas which are dominated by knobthorn acacia, marula, sicklebush and bushwillow. The main road consists of the tarred H1-2 but there are a number of short gravel turnoffs leading to waterholes and other scenic points, all making for a rewarding day of sightseeing. In addition to plentiful impala, kudu, baboon and a variety of other animals, your chances of seeing lion and buffalo along this route are good and perhaps even leopard if you're lucky. Graceful giraffe and stunning sable antelope are also regular sights.

Near Skukuza, a slow drive over the **Sabie River** causeway rarely fails to yield some interesting sightings. Best of all is the highly pleasing view of the tree-lined river with its smoothly eroded boulders and clumps of reeds which just beg to be photographed. Looking west, you will see the landmark **Selati Railway Bridge** straddling the river, an architecturally pleasing structure which evokes many adventures of the early history of the Park. A sandbank on the same side of the river more often than not hosts an enormous crocodile which, for several years, has made this its home, silently sharing its favoured daytime roost with a younger crocodile basking nearby. Egyptian geese strut about in the shallow water and – if you look carefully – you'll see **Labeo** and other fish lazily mouthing the rocks for particles of food. On the other side of the bridge, pied wagtails with pumped up chests and flicking tails regularly swagger on the rocks, while a terrapin quietly suns itself close to the water's edge. These are magic moments which will remain in your memory.

Four kilometres (2½ miles) further you reach the **Sand River** causeway. All that remains of this once majestic river is a narrow rush of sparkling water gurgling its way between time-smoothed granite boulders but the wide expanse of sand and banks of reeds are attractive. Hamerkop birds with their wedge-shaped heads often perch near the water's edge, ready to pounce on some unsuspecting frog or other tasty morsel. The road further parallels the Sand River for some distance, and leopard are regularly seen in the riverine thickets which cover much of the river's edge. One of the most unforgettable sights anyone could hope for is to find a leopard draped lazily over the branch of a tree, occasionally lifting its head to calmly survey its surrounds with half-open eyes.

Above: *Beautiful Egyptian geese are among the numerous waterfowl making their homes alongside the river.*
Below: *Draped languidly over a branch, a leopard waits for dusk to begin its nocturnal hunting.*

Above: *Giraffe make fascinating photographic subjects as they awkwardly drink from Matimahle Dam.*
Below: *The surefooted, shy klipspringer, an antelope rarely seen in the Park.*

Travelling on towards Tshokwane, you reach the **Matimahle dam** which is only a short distance off the main road. From the shade of the huge marula trees you can soak up the peaceful bushveld atmosphere and enjoy the sounds of birds providing a continuous background chorus. Giraffe are regular visitors here and they make wonderful photographic subjects either when they stoop with widely splayed legs to gently sip at the water's surface or stretch their long necks to reach some tasty leaves well out of reach of lesser animals.

Travelling further will bring you to a series of rocky hills and here you should look around carefully for **klipspringer** usually poised motionless on the rocks. They are shy animals and very territorial so only one pair and sometimes their young offspring will be found on a

TSHOKWANE

This was the name of a **Sotho**-tribesman who lived here in historical times. Tshokwane is one of the most popular picnic sites in Kruger, partly because it lies on the game-rich Skukuza-Satara route, but also because of its excellent facilities. The large tree around which the roof has been built is a sausage tree, the roof being partly for shade but also in order to prevent the heavy fruits from dropping on people!

particular hill. These fascinating animals superficially resemble steenbuck but are adapted for rocky outcrops where they can nimbly jump from boulder to boulder with amazing surefootedness! Attached to one of the huge granite rocks is a memorial plaque commemorating the **Orpen** couple who donated large tracts of farmland for inclusion into Kruger. Across the road nearby is another plaque commemorating **Paul Kruger** and here you can get out to stretch your legs while walking up a gentle slope to read the inscription.

Approaching Tshokwane you will find two waterholes popular with visitors because they often yield unexpected sightings. First is **Leeupan**, very rich in birdlife especially during the wet months of summer. During this season a substantial marsh develops which attracts a good range of ducks, geese and storks. A little further you reach **Shiloweni dam**, a wide expanse of water usually with some hippo resting, waiting for the heat of the day to pass before they venture out to forage for grass in the cool darkness. This is also a favoured site of waterbuck, mostly seen as a single dominant bull easily recognized by its massive sweeping horns, accompanied by a group of females and some immatures. Within the cleared parking area, a few cheeky plovers and starlings strut about demanding to be fed, tempting you to ignore regulations which forbid this. Lion are often seen at or near this dam, lazing in the shade in easy photographing distance.

> **KRUGER MILLIONS!**
>
> In early decades, rumours were rife that on his way to permanent exile at the turn of the century, Transvaal Republic President, Paul Kruger, ordered a massive booty of treasure to be hidden somewhere in or near what is now the southern Kruger Park. As Warden of the then **Sabi Game Reserve**, Colonel James Stevenson Hamilton had to fend off numerous requests from fortune seekers who wished to unearth these so-called **Kruger millions**. Among other places, the rocky outcrops near Tshokwane were extensively searched for this alleged hidden bounty.

Below: *Visitors can stretch their legs by walking to the Paul Kruger Memorial Plaque between Skukuza and Tshokwane.*

After 43km (27 miles) of excellent game-viewing, you reach **Tshokwane Picnic Spot**. This is the biggest and best-equipped picnic area in Kruger and you can buy a variety of refreshments here. Tshokwane has great atmosphere, more vibrant and lively than the calm and laid-back feel associated with all the other picnic sites. Part of the reason has to be the numerous starlings which chase around the picnic grounds, loudly and arrogantly pecking at scraps of

Above: *The Kruger Park's best-equipped picnic spot at Tshokwane is wonderfully vibrant and lively.*

leftover food. Tshokwane overlooks the usually dry Nwaswitsontso River, its banks intermittently dotted with beautifully spreading wild date palms festooned with large clusters of yellow fruits during February to April.

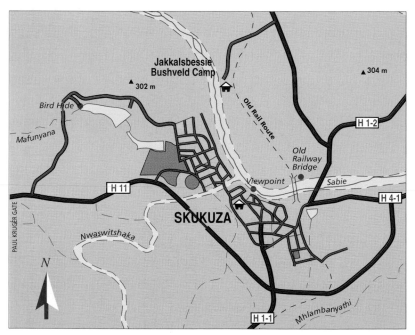

Skukuza to Renosterkoppies **

A little-known gem of a road lies to the south of
Skukuza in prime bushveld, and leading to some exceptionally scenic points and often resulting in sightings of
rhino, lion and wild dog. The route is a relatively short
41km (25 miles) round trip but you should budget for at
least two hours because of the various get-out points
where you may want to relax for a while and appreciate
the excellent scenery.

The initial stretch is along the tarred **Napi Road** (H1-1)
which has many impala and is also good for kudu and
giraffe with occasional sightings of ground hornbills,
always fascinating to watch! Six kilometres (4 miles) after
leaving Skukuza you turn left onto a good quality gravel
road (S114) which winds through somewhat arid veld
dominated by tall marula and knobthorn trees. This is
where you should look for rhino and wild dog which
inhabit this area. In late afternoon or early morning hyena
and lion are also regularly seen. With so many 'quality
sightings' it remains a mystery why this road is not far
more popular with visitors. Perhaps the idea of a gravel
road turns many away but with so little traffic, dust is
really not a problem!

FRUSTRATING FLIES

Several 'fly-belts' – broad
swaths of bush in which
tsetse fly were confined –
frustrated the efforts of 19th
century pioneers to freely
colonize the Lowveld. In an
otherwise arid country, the
Sabie River and Crocodile
River were obvious water-rich
routes for transport riders
using ox-wagons to convey
goods from mining towns
to the Mozambique coast.
Tsetse flies like cattle blood
and transmitted parasites
resulted in large-scale cattle
losses. This was a major
contributory reason for
the railway line to be built
in the late 19th century. The
massive Rinderpest outbreak
of 1896 wiped out vast
numbers of game and
cattle but also resulted in the
disappearance of tsetse fly.

Left: *Loping on its
unfortunate frame, the
spotted hyena has the
strongest jaws in the
animal kingdom.*

Above: *From the Stevenson-Hamilton lookout point one is greeted by a magnificent view of the entire southern Kruger Park.*
Opposite top: *Playful baboons frequent the Renosterkoppie hills, providing wonderful entertainment for tourists.*
Opposite bottom: *For atmospheric splendour and a panoramic view, visit Mathekenyane Hill in the late afternoon.*

After 6km (4 miles) along the S114, you turn right for a short ride to a hilltop lookout point which will almost certainly prove a highlight. This is the **Stevenson-Hamilton Hill**, a conglomerate of huge granite boulders over which not only the ashes of 'The Colonel' were strewn but also those of his wife, Hilda. From the parking area you walk around a particularly impressive rock – against which a **memorial plaque** is fixed – to be greeted on the other side by a magnificent view over the entire southern Kruger National Park. Far to the southwest you can even see the well-known landmark **Legogote Mountain** which is well outside the Park in the direction of the town of White River. It's a splendid scene and one where you will want to linger for a while to enjoy the atmosphere.

Slightly south of Stevenson-Hamilton Hill is another cluster of hills known as **Renosterkoppies** which is Afrikaans for 'Rhino hills'. There is also a waterhole which is regularly visited by rhino (hence the name) as well as other animals such as lion, hyena and a good number of impala. The hills are a favourite night-time roost for **baboons** and if you drive there in the late afternoon you are sure to see them gambolling about the clifftops.

Veering westwards will take you to the tarred H3 which links up with the main H1-1 again to take you back to Skukuza. At the junction of these two main

roads there are two sets of rocky koppies and if you look carefully you might see the pair of klipspringer which claim these hills as their territory. They are lovely, graceful animals which make stunning photographs especially when you see them poised atop a rock. Along the way back to Skukuza there is a short turnoff to **Mathekenyane Hill** (previously called 'Grano Kop') which provides an all-round panoramic view of the surrounding bushveld. Try to be here in the late afternoon, at which time the scene is quite breathtaking.

3
The Southern Region

The 'Southern Region' refers to the area between the Sabie and **Crocodile rivers**, and is about one-fifth of the total area of the Park. This is lion country and it also has a higher density of rhino than anywhere else in the Park! Several excellent drives – especially those in the general area around Lower Sabie – combine exceptional scenery with a rich mixture of game. Much of the area is fairly densely vegetated with a diverse mix of trees, the most notable species being **knobthorn** and other **acacia's**, **marula**, **bushwillow combretum**, **leadwood**, **sicklebush**, and **silver-leaf terminalia**, while the riversides are dominated by enormous **Sycamore figs** and densely-crowned **jackalberries**. Annual rainfall is highest around Pretoriuskop and is reflected by the tall grass and dense cover of terminalia trees and magnificent stands of **kiaat teak**. Only in the east near the **Lebombo Mountains** does the terrain become more open. Aside from the two major rivers already mentioned, a number of other seasonal rivers add habitat for riverine-associated birds and animals. **Craggy hills** characterize the area between Malelane and Pretoriuskop, while in contrast the eastern section bordering the Lebombo Mountains tends to be very flat, giving one a feeling of being in almost limitless savanna. The southern region offers you the best chances of seeing both black and white rhino, while the best **game-viewing** is in the grassy flatland between Lower Sabie and Crocodile Bridge. Large camps in this region include Skukuza, Pretoriuskop, Berg-en-Dal and Lower Sabie.

DON'T MISS

*** Lower Sabie Camp: full amenities and excellent base for game-viewing.
*** Lower Sabie to Crocodile Bridge drive: excellent for spotting lion, buffalo and rhino.
** Biyamlti Camp: secluded privacy, great atmosphere with lots of game.
** Nkuhlu Picnic Spot: overlooking the Sabie River, with good amenities and great atmosphere.

Opposite: *One of the Park's best camps, Lower Sabie, situated on the banks of the Sabie River, is an excellent base for game-viewing.*

LOWER SABIE ★★★

If you want to be based in the South for a day or two, Lower Sabie is recommended as the camp of choice because of the plentiful game in the area, combined with easy viewing and magnificent scenery. Highly recommended as your base while touring the Southern Region, this is a lush, highly pleasant camp scenically arranged along the lower reaches of the Sabie River. It is conveniently placed in the middle of excellent game-viewing country, with the possibility of many rewarding drives in the immediate vicinity. Neatly kept, extensive lawns and abundant trees providing shade, give the camp an atmosphere of a luxuriant oasis amidst the usually hot and rather dry bushveld. You will enjoy this camp with its magnificent river front – regularly attracting buffalo and many other animals to drink within easy viewing distance, as well as the numerous starlings, sparrows, doves and grey loeries chattering and cooing in the background.

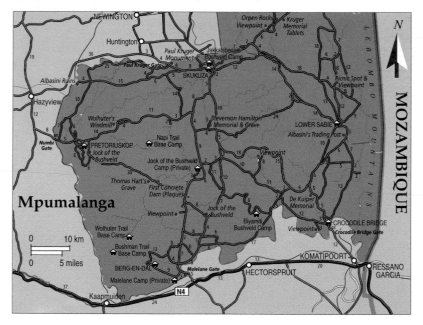

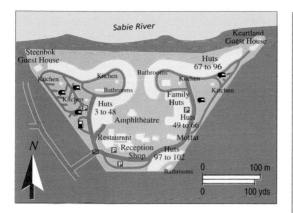

Lower Sabie can accommodate about 147 visitors in huts or cottages, while the camping area – serviced by kitchen units and ablution blocks – has stands for 28 tents or caravans. This makes it a medium-sized camp, offering good facilities but without the atmosphere of a large, overcrowded camp. There is a restaurant, cafeteria, and a shop supplying virtually everything you are likely to need, as well as a fuel station. Lower Sabie has a very relaxed, friendly atmosphere and is one of the most pleasant camps to stay in.

Highlights of Lower Sabie

Lower Sabie is the kind of camp where, if you're in the mood, you could easily spend a pleasant day simply lounging around the camp, strolling through the lush camp scenery, admiring the birds, having tea or lunch on the covered verandah adjoining the restaurant, or spreading a blanket under a shady tree and reading a book. You are guaranteed to unwind and relax here.

There are a number of excellent drives starting from Lower Sabie, combining good game-viewing with magnificent scenery. Two of the Park's finest routes give you the best opportunity for seeing lion, rhino and a good range of all the animals that occur in this part of the Kruger National Park. For something 'different', you can go on one of the regular **night drives**, which

BRAILLE TRAIL

A thoughtful concept, the special trail in Berg-en-Dal camp gives blind people the opportunity to tangibly experience nature. This 'Braille Trail' meanders along the river-end of camp, with a cable as guide, using bronze Braille plaques to provide information. You stop at several places to touch and feel the texture of the bark of different trees, and there are also skulls of elephant, rhino and buffalo to explore. Tape recordings are available at the Information Centre (near the shop) which you can take with you to further enrich this Trail experience.

Opposite: *Berg-en-Dal in the extreme south, one of Kruger's larger camps, is pleasantly landscaped to maximize open space and natural vegetation.*

gives you an excellent chance of seeing hyena, genet, civet cat and many other night animals which you are unlikely to see by day. Or else go on a guided **day drive**, which takes you at least partly on roads you would normally not have access to, and your guide will provide commentary and insights into animal life you'll be seeing around you. Enquire at the Reception Office about these **night drives** and **day drives**, which are in open-sided trucks and have proved to be very popular.

If you have the inclination, you could drive to Skukuza for the day where there are some facilities not available anywhere else in the Park.

OTHER CAMPS IN THE SOUTHERN REGION
Berg-en-Dal ★★

Located in the extreme south near Malelane town this spaciously arranged Main camp is cradled among some of the highest hills to be found in the Park. This is good habitat for the mountain reedbuck which aren't found anywhere else in Kruger. With about 300 beds available, it is one of the larger camps, and has been deliberately landscaped to retain considerable open space and natural vegetation within the camp. It has an extensive camping area, swimming pool, cafeteria and a restaurant which overlooks a nearby dam, conference facility, fuel station, launderette, large shop, public telephone and a Braille Trail for blind people.

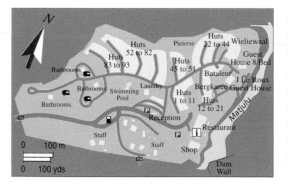

There is also an **Information Centre** near the shop. This centre has an interesting static display which you might want to have a look at. More importantly, though, the Information Officer is there to help answer any questions which you might have about recent sightings of lion, rhino or

other animals which you can then try to locate. Try to arrange one of the camp's rangers to take you on the so-called 'rhino trail' inside Berg-en-Dal camp. During this walk the ranger will point out interesting trees, plants, birds, lizards and so on. The Matjulu stream has been dammed in front of the restaurant and is home to numerous terrapins, with birds plentiful and elephant sometimes coming in for a daytime drink.

Crocodile Bridge *

This Main camp borders the Crocodile River in the southeastern corner of the Park near Komatipoort town, and is fairly small. It has 20 huts, each with three beds, kitchen, air-conditioner, shower and toilet. There is a small camping area as well. The camp serves as an Entrance or Exit Gate to the south which is the road joining the National N4 highway at Komatipoort 13km away (8 miles). But when the heavy summer rains flood the low-level causeway the entrance to this camp ceases to exist! Crocodile Bridge has a fuel station, a small shop offering tinned foods and basic items, a laundrette and a public telephone.

> **HIPPO HAUNT**
>
> A short 8km (5 mile) drive from Crocodile Bridge brings you to the **Hippo Pool**. A ranger will escort you during the brief walk down to the river, where good photographs can usually be taken of the many hippo in the pool. Back at the parking area is a **Bushman painting** which dates back several hundred years.

Bathrooms   Reception

Kitchen
Bathrooms

Huts 19+20

Staff

Huts 1 to 18

0   50 m

0   50 yds

MUD BRICKS

On 1 May 1813 an 18-year-old **João Albasini** found himself stranded in Mozambique after his ship was stranded off that coast. He soon became a highly respected trader and elephant hunter. The first white man to settle in the Transvaal Lowveld and, from 1846 to 1848, he kept a store – named **Magashulaskraal** – near the present-day Pretoriuskop Camp. The partly restored ruins with artefacts and information posters can be accessed from the S1 road north of Pretoriuskop.

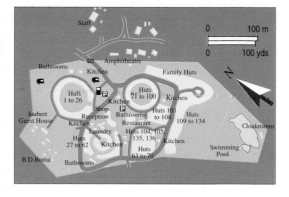

Below: Pretoriuskop Camp in the southwestern region is an excellent base for viewing rhino, but is away from the main game-viewing areas.

Pretoriuskop *

One of the oldest in the Park, this camp offered the first accomodation available to tourists in the late-1920s. It lies in the southwestern corner of Kruger in a high rainfall zone, an excellent base for viewing rhino and perhaps even rare Lichtenstein's hartebeest. A large camp, with some 360 beds and a spacious camping area, it is tucked away from the main game-viewing areas, so seldom bustles with activity. The atmosphere is pleasant and it has a large swimming pool – partly built around natural granite boulders – popular with children. There is a small restaurant and large shop, well-stocked with curios. The camp has a fuel station, cafeteria, laundrette and public telephones. The 'Sable Trail' which winds through a large part of the camp is quite clearly marked by cemented sable spoor. Brochures are available at the Reception Office and these, together with the various information boards along the Sable Trail, provide much insight into the medicinal values of some of the trees and plants found in camp, as well as other interesting historical facts associated with Pretoriuskop.

Byamiti **

Set in dense bushveld overlooking the Byamiti River (dry much of the year) and liberally adorned with many tall jackalberry and other trees, this Bushveld camp has a very relaxed and pleasant atmosphere. It can accommodate 70 people in 15 bungalows. The surrounding area provides good opportunities for seeing lion and a wide range of other animals including buffalo and rhino.

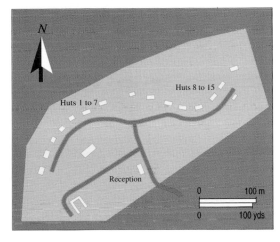

Jock of the Bushveld *

Midway between Skukuza and Malelane, this secluded Private camp overlooks the dry but scenic Mntomene riverbed. Enormous jackalberry and other trees provide abundant shade. The old transport route along which ox-wagons trundled their way between Lydenburg and Delagoa Bay (Maputo Bay) passed nearby, and the wagon-wheels and other historical items exhibited here conjure up images of those pioneering days. The camp can take 12 people, has wonderful atmosphere, and is surrounded by excellent game-country.

Malelane *

This camp has been retained as a relic of the original Malelane rest camp of earlier years. It can accommodate 19 people and, unlike any of the other Private camps, it has air-conditioning in the huts. It is near Berg-en-Dal camp, Malelane Entrance Gate and Malelane town. Game-viewing in the area is reasonably good, but its main advantage is the easy access to the N4 highway which links Johannesburg and Maputo.

COURAGEOUS COMPANION

In 1907 Percy FitzPatrick published the book *Jock of the Bushveld* which has reached the hearts of thousands of people ever since. The son of an Irish Judge, the young Percy left his comfortable home to become a transport rider in the 1880s, moving freight by ox-wagon from coastal Lourenço Marques (Maputo) to the mining towns of Barberton and Lydenburg. He was given a leftover puppy, which soon proved to be exceptionally intelligent, tough and loyal. The story is about the shared experiences of hunting, hardship and humour between this man and his faithful dog. FitzPatrick later went on to become involved in national politics, and was later knighted.

Jakkalsbessie **

It is a small Bushveld camp, situated near the airport
about 7km (5 miles) from Skukuza. The camp was initial-
ly intended as a retreat for government ministers and
other VIPs but is now available to everyone. It can sleep
32 people in eight family cottages and has conference
facilities with all the necessary projection and other
equipment. Despite its proximity to the airport and
Skukuza (which is an advantage for many people), it has
managed to retain a 'wilderness' atmosphere, largely
due to the slowly-flowing river in front of the camp and
the many trees interspersed between the cottages. So you
can fly in to Skukuza and within 15 minutes of arrival
ensconce yourself in your own private bit of bushveld,
complete with river frontage!

BEST DRIVES
Lower Sabie to Crocodile Bridge ***

The eastern plain adjoining the Lebombo Mountains
between Lower Sabie and Crocodile Bridge is a marvellous tapestry of varying landscapes each with its own
beauty and lavish complement of wildlife. Most rewarding is the gravel **S28** road which takes you through
highly scenic grassy savanna rich in zebra, giraffe, rhino
and lion. Tall knobthorn acacias and ever-graceful
marula trees abound and provide welcome shade for
herds of kudu and impala, while dainty
steenbuck also find refuge from the
blistering sun. The craggy cliffs of
the Lebombos are ever-present and
dominate the eastern horizon.

Shortly after leaving Lower Sabie
camp you will find the high-level bridge
crossing the Sabie River. It's a brief
detour off your main route, but well
worth the extra few minutes. Despite
being an obnoxious exotic weed which
so far has tenaciously resisted all efforts
at eradication, the lush carpet of clover-
leafed floating **water cabbage** plants

Below: *A pair of adult
giraffe browse on the flowers
of the tall knobthorn tree.*

covering much of the dam makes a glorious appearance. It forms a platform
on which a number of stilt-legged
jacana birds can always be seen pecking away at bits of food. Elsewhere at
the fringes of the reeds shy black crane
warily search the rocky stream edge for
titbits, while pied and giant kingfishers
perch on the dam wall intently peering
into the crystal water for a careless fish.
The birds are tame and allow you to
approach fairly close for photographs.

Almost midway along the S28 route you will reach
the **Nhlanganzwani Dam**, a soothing oasis rarely
without animals coming in to slake their thirst or browse
on the trees nearby. Giraffe and graceful waterbuck are
common sights here, peering unconcerned at occasional
herds of zebra which stir up eddies of dust in their
zestful play near the water's edge. This is also where
you should keep a sharp lookout for lion which tend to
concentrate in the area.

Duke Windmill is also a favoured drinking hole
for many animals and lion are regularly seen resting
in the shade of nearby trees. Starlings and other birds
provide an almost incessant background chatter. Doves
of various species abound, and during the summer the
magnificent plumage of lilac-breasted rollers never fails
to attract your attention.

Above: *River-crossings are
excellent for viewing herons,
ducks and many other birds,
but lilac-breasted rollers
prefer the open plains.*

Slightly to the west the tarred **H4-2**, also known as the
Gomondwane road, travels through far more dense
countryside dominated by thickets of Delagoa thorn
(*Acacia welwitschii*). This is a favourite food for animals
such as giraffe, impala and kudu, while buffalo and rhino
like the cover which these thickets provide. The **Vurhami
Spruit** twists and winds its way close to the road for a
long stretch near Crocodile Bridge, and this section is
particularly rewarding. Kudu, impala and a good range
of other animals are plentiful and your chances of seeing
lion and buffalo are excellent. The proximity of water and
dense bush also means that birds are abundant.

PATHFINDER

Forming the boundary
between the Kruger and
Mozambique, the scenic
Lebombo Mountains extend
further south through
Swaziland and into KwaZulu-
Natal. The name is derived
from the Swazi term **ama-
bombo**, meaning 'direction or
bearings one takes on jour-
neying', implying that these
mountains were used as a
directional reference.

Pretoriuskop to Malelane **

This route, following the H2-2 to Afsaal Picnic Spot and then the H3 to Malelane, is the top drive in Kruger for seeing white rhino. The diverse mix of bushveld and, in particular, the moderate density of the vegetation creates an ideal habitat for these animals. But you will also find other game along the way, including a possibility of seeing breathtaking sable antelope. The males are exquisite animals, with enormous sweeping horns arching back over the body. Even more rare Lichtenstein's hartebeest – offspring of stock originally reintroduced from Malawi during the 1980s – also frequent the area near Pretoriuskop. To top it all, the area near Malelane and Berg-en-Dal is the only part of the Park where you are likely to see highly localized mountain reedbuck and 'common' reedbuck. To keep your hopes up during the search for these rarities, kudu, giraffe, zebra, impala and many smaller animals such as steenbok are frequent sights along the way, all forming prey for lion which are regularly seen here.

The gravel H2-2, also known as the **Voortrekker Road**, refers to the pioneering explorers who traversed this area with oxwagons during the early 19th century in search of a route to Delagoa Bay (now Maputo Bay). Several lonely graves marked by small piles of stones in otherwise endless bush still attest to the hardships caused by malaria, lions, tsetse flies and a harsh, unforgiving bush.

Right: *Lichtenstein's hartebeest, one of the rarest antelope, can be seen in the area near Pretoriuskop.*
Opposite: *Resembling a capsized ship's hull, the remarkable Ship Mountain never fails to raise curiosity.*

Travelling from Pretoriuskop you soon reach **Ship Mountain**, a remarkable solitary hill resembling the upturned hull of a ship. While the general countryside surrounding the hill bears relatively few visible surface rocks, Ship Mountain is a massive conglomerate of boulders, a striking contrast which never fails to raise curiosity. The area here holds numerous rhino and you should look carefully among the patches of scrubby *Combretum Terminalia* and sicklebush trees. Despite their bulk, the inconspicuous grey hide of these animals blends remarkably well with surrounding clumps of scrub.

Afsaal Picnic Spot is a convenient midway stop at the junction of the H2-2 and H3 roads. It has a little kiosk which serves tea and other refreshments, which you can enjoy in the shade of one of the trees. Near you will be a giant jackalberry tree growing from the side of a long-disused termite pyramid. Parks officials have put up an illustrated poster here which provides some information on the fascinating lives of these insects. For some years now a small colony of dwarf mongooses has made its home near the picnic site, the hyperactive little animals becoming fairly tame and allowing you to take photographs during one of their scavenging visits.

PRETORIUSKOP

This was the very first camp offering accommodation for visitors. It was named after Willem Pretorius — buried in this area — a member of the 1848 Carl Trichardt expedition to Delagoa Bay.

DRY-DOCK

Not far from Pretoriuskop lies **Ship Mountain**, a massive pile of loose rocks, unlike most other hills in the area. The hill looks like a capsized ship with its hull rearing above the surface. It forms part of a narrow underground geological intrusion termed **gabbro** which extends northwest from Malelane towards Hazyview. Occasional outcrops give rise to koppies such as Ship Mountain.

Approaching Malelane the land becomes much more hilly and this is where you should keep an eye out for mountain reedbuck. Rhino and elephant also occur here, as do a wide range of the more usual kudu, impala and others. Along the way you will cross some riverbeds which usually only have water during the rainy summer months. Tall jackalberry and other trees line the edges and are favourite perches for large raptors such as martial eagles, always an impressive sight with their regal pose and stern gaze. Some lucky visitors are also startled to find an unexpected leopard draped lazily over a shaded branch, calmly waiting for nightfall to hunt for food!

Skukuza to Malelane ★★★

Although there are two roads (H3 and S114) leading almost parallel to each other to Malelane, the gravel **S114** is far more rewarding, having a wonderful atmosphere and several highly enjoyable loop roads which wind along streams always yielding some surprises. With detours, the route is 71km (44 miles) and will probably take about three hours to complete.

Near Skukuza you can detour briefly to enjoy the splendid scenery from the viewpoint halfway up the **Stevenson-Hamilton Hill**. If you have binoculars, see if you can recognize Ship Mountain near Pretoriuskop and the prominent Legogote Mountain well outside the

Right: *The scenery from Stevenson-Hamilton Hill is well worth the drive.*

Park towards White River town; scanning the open plain below through your binoculars will almost certainly also reveal some animals.

The highlight for many people travelling along this route is the all-too-brief 14km (9 miles) **S23** loop road which meanders closely alongside the **Biyamiti River**. Although the river is mostly dry, its broad sandy bed with scattered patches of reeds, rocks and palms is highly scenic and the banks have fairly dense stands of tall and evergreen tree fuchsias, jackalberry and many others. Buffalo, rhino and elephant are regularly seen here, together with kudu, impala, zebra, warthog and a wide range of birds. Soon after rejoining the S114 you cross the Biyamiti River. Take your time crossing the bridge – the reedbeds, rock accumulations and pools of water always have something to rouse your interest. The pool on the southern side is especially rewarding, either with kingfishers, green-backed herons or some other birds quietly strutting about the matted weeds. When you've crossed the river, watch for klipspringer on the rocky hill.

Instead of following the S114 to its eventual junction with the tarred H3, turn off onto the **S118** which twists along the **Mlambane River**. Although only 8km (5 miles) in length, this stretch of road never fails to yield something of interest. The scenery is good and you regularly come across herds of impala, zebra, occasional kudu, perhaps even buffalo, rhino or elephant – if luck is on your side.

Above: *White rhino graze near the Biyamiti River, an area popular with buffalo and even elephant. One can see the extensive damage to the bark of the trees caused by elephants.*

LANDMARK FRAUD

When the Transvaal government in 1890 approved the concept of a railway line traversing what is now the southern Kruger Park, several parties immediately competed for the contract. Gross misrepresentations of competence and bribery were common. The government eventually stopped the chaotic fiasco in 1894 after 120km (75 miles) of line had been laid from Komatipoort to Newington slightly north of Skukuza. A sturdy bridge over the Sabie River – a major landmark visible from Skukuza camp – was built in 1910 and the Selati Line to Tzaneen was finally completed in 1912.

4
The Central Region

This is the most game-rich area and includes some of the best scenery anywhere in Kruger. Spend three days driving around this region and you will be quite enchanted by the Park. Known as the Central Region, it stretches from the Sabie River northwards to the Olifants River. It includes the vast grass-filled plains around Satara which are referred to as the **Central Plains**. Giraffe, zebra and wildebeest abound, their numbers allowing an exceptionally high density of lion to prosper. Stately marula and leadwood trees provide shade for the wandering herds of elephant, while the occasional cheetah surveys its hunting ground from the vantage point atop a termite mound. To the east, the craggy **Lebombo Mountains** rear up as a solid line to form a natural boundary with Mozambique, while the extreme west and south are more dense and provide habitat for a greater variety of animals, including sable, rhino, buffalo, even an occasional roan, eland or pack of wild dogs. Game-viewing is excellent anywhere in the Central Region, but some of the very best drives are those leading from Satara to Nwanetsi (gravel road along Nwanetsi River), from Satara to Olifants along the Gudzane/Bangu gravel road, and from Satara via the Timbavati road to Olifants. As Satara is so ideally situated in the centre of the prime game-viewing area, offering a particularly scenic and enjoyable stay, this camp is highly recommended as a base for your stay in the Central Region. Other camps in the region are all small, such as Orpen, Talamati, Roodewal and Nwanetsi.

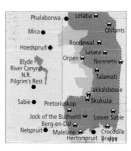

DON'T MISS

*** Talamati Bushveld Camp: near Orpen Gate, this camp is an unappreciated gem! Wonderful atmosphere and a wide range of birds.
** Nwanetsi picnic spot: great for late afternoon sundowners. Fabulous hilltop views.
* Open-air amphitheatre: showing many fascinating wildlife films.
* Satara: easy access to the best game-viewing areas of the Central Region.

Opposite: *The lovely spacious layout of Satara camp is one of its many popular drawcards.*

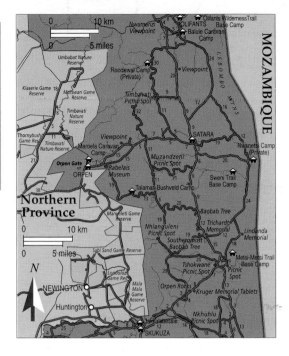

Below: *Probably the best camp in the Kruger, Satara allows access to the ultimate wildlife areas, has excellent amenities and exudes a relaxed bushveld charm despite its large size.*

SATARA ★★★

Perfectly located to give easy access to the best game-viewing areas of the Central Region, Satara is the perfect choice as base camp while touring this part of the Park. It is a large camp with open spaces, tall trees, an abundance of birdlife, and plenty of wonderful atmosphere. Large numbers of starlings, buffalo weavers and house sparrows fly about between the huts in search of crumbs. Here you can relax in comfort. It can accommodate 441 people in huts or cottages, making it the second biggest camp in Kruger. There is also a large camping area with ablution blocks and open-air kitchens.

Adjoining the camp Reception Office is a well-stocked shop, restaurant, cafeteria, and a sweeping verandah where you can enjoy snacks or drinks in the company of birds flying onto your table. A fuel station, launderette and **Automobile Association vehicle repair facility** are available. There is also an open-air amphitheatre for wildlife film shows on some evenings (enquire at Reception), with an attached small display room where photographs of the old Satara and information on wildlife are on view. Joggers will enjoy this camp as its considerable size allows a variation of routes to be followed.

Highlights of Satara

The exceptionally **abundant wildlife** of the Central Region is in itself a highlight, with a high likelihood of seeing lion, buffalo, elephant, rhino, leopard and cheetah. The **scenery** too, especially the close-up views of the Lebombo Mountains, the craggy hills near Roodewal, and the seemingly endless plains, are all highly pleasing, making your stay in this area probably the main highlight of your Kruger trip.

Staying in **Satara** is also a highlight, the rich mix of rollers, orioles, weavers and other **birdlife** a constant source of amusement and pleasure, and the relaxing atmosphere of the camp a soothing experience. Ask about wildlife **film shows** and **day/night drives** at the camp reception office. There are several drives from Satara which are unrivalled in the Park for seeing wildlife. Those include the **Nwanetsi/Tshokwane route**, and that along the **Timbavati River**; all highly recommended. Few people will fail to be impressed by the fabulous view from the **Nwanetsi Lookout Point** which allows you a rather splendid panoramic view of the Central Plain, the Lebombo Mountains and a peaceful riverine scene below.

> **TOP STOPS**
>
> Aside from the **Nwanetsi picnic spot**, there are several other places well worth seeing. These include **Nsemani dam** (on the H7 to Orpen), **Girivane dam** at the junction of the S12 and S40 roads, **Kumana dam** (on the H1-3 to Tshokwane), and **Shiloweni dam** south of Tshokwane. Places where you may leave your vehicle include **Tshokwane picnic site**, which is highly recommended as a rest-stop where you can buy tea or other refreshments. Not far from Tshokwane is the **Orpen dam** lookout point, with toilets, cool-drinks for sale and a shaded resting area which has a great view over the dam below and the hills beyond.

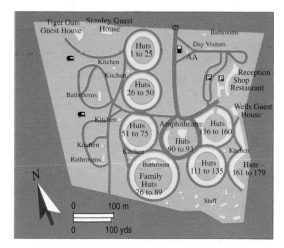

Tiger Oats Guest House — Stanley Guest House — Bathrooms — Day Visitors — AA — Reception, Shop, Restaurant — Wells Guest House — Huts 1 to 25 — Kitchen — Kitchen — Huts 26 to 50 — Bathrooms — Kitchen — Huts 51 to 75 — Amphitheatre — Huts 136 to 160 — Huts 90 to 93 — Kitchen — Kitchen — Huts 111 to 135 — Huts 161 to 179 — Kitchen — Bathrooms — Bathroom — Family Huts 76 to 89 — Staff — N — 0 100 m — 0 100 yds

Other camps in the Central Region
Orpen *

Set on the western border of the Park, Orpen is a small Main camp and serves as Entrance Gate to the Central Region. There is no restaurant and the small shop stocks only the bare essentials. There is a pleasant shady area with barbecue facilities where day visitors can picnic and there is an ablution block nearby. There are lots of birds flying around the many trees livening up the camp. Orpen offers about 30 beds and a fuel station. Most people drive straight through in their eagerness to get well into the Park, but the camp is in many ways an ideal base for game-viewing. From your comfortable fire-side seat you can listen to lion roaring at night, or by day take any of the various roads in the area for splendid sights and scenes. Best of all, and conveniently close to Orpen, is the highly rewarding Timbavati route, one of the very best drives anywhere in the Park!

Marula *

Marula is only 4km (2½ miles) from Orpen Camp and is tucked into dense bushveld which fringes the banks of the Timbavati River. Marula is a small facility which caters only for caravaners and campers.

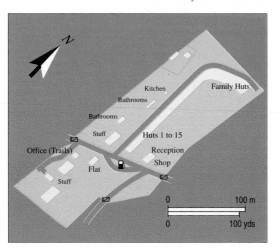

The camp has a kitchen-unit with cooking facilities, a communal refrigerator and a large ablution block. Unfortunately there is no shop, fuel station or other facilities available. It's rather rustic with a great 'get-in-touch-with-nature' atmosphere. If this is what you're looking for then Marula is the obvious choice. It will be necessary for you to provide your own accomodation, be it a tent or caravan.

Balule *

Close to the low-level causeway over the Olifants River, Balule by virtue of its locality falls into the Central Region but is actually a satellite unit of Olifants camp. If you intend staying at Balule you will have to check in at Olifants first. With only six three-bed huts and an attached camping area with 15 stands, it adjoins the Olifants River about 11km (7 miles) from Olifants Camp. Take note that there is no electricity in this camp and lanterns are used at night. The huts do not have their own toilets or showers, so you will have to use the communal ablution facilities (which are ample and clean). There are two refrigerators with limited space for keeping your perishable items. You either love Balule or you hate it, but it is very popular with a small core of 'get-back-to-basics' enthusiasts.

Talamati ***

Set in a good game-viewing area on the western side of the Park near Orpen Gate, this Bushveld camp is an unappreciated gem! It lies cosily sprawled along the southern bank of the Nwaswitsontso River, which, although mostly dry, is lined with many magnificent jackalberry and other trees providing shade and resting sites for a wide range of birds. Talamati can accommodate 80 people in well-spaced, highly-comfortable cottages. There is a raised hide near the entrance gate which overlooks a watering hole, a lovely site to relax with a sundowner while watching some animals coming in for a final drink. You won't regret spending some time here. Lion are plentiful in the surrounding area and you are almost guaranteed to hear their distant roars while slumbering in the comfort of your bed.

VIEWPOINTS

On top of a cliff overlooking the **Sweni River**, the lookout point at **Nwanetsi picnic site** is second only to Olifants camp as the most scenic viewpoint in Kruger. To the east, the *Euphorbia*-clad Lebombos fill the horizon while southwards and westwards the open plains stretch as far as the eye can see. Below the viewpoint there is a small natural dam, with *Nymphaea* lilies floating on the quiet water. Waterbirds are common. At the under-cover parking area are toilets, a spacious barbecue area with shaded tables and chairs, and cool-drinks for sale. The picnic site is a short distance from **Nwanetsi camp**, about one and a half hour's drive from Satara.

Below: *A raised hide overlooking the waterhole at Talamati, an excellent spot for sundowners while viewing game.*

Above: *Best of the private camps, Roodewal is situated next to the Timbavati River in one of the best game-viewing areas in the Park.*

Nwanetsi ★★★

Being at the edge of the renowned Central Plains, Nwanetsi is one of the best-located Private camps for game viewing, close to abundant herds of zebra, wildebeest, giraffe and many other animals. Aside from the fantastic views of the *Euphorbia*-clad Lebombo Mountains (really just overgrown hills, but nevertheless very scenic), you are almost certain to hear either lion roaring at night or the eerie calls of hyena. All the roads in the area are excellent for game-viewing. You are also close enough to the Nwanetsi picnic spot to have a late-afternoon sundowner there and absorb the absolutely majestic scene which unfolds from your hilltop viewpoint, before returning to camp less than 2km (1 mile) away! Beware of scorpions here, they are plentiful and you get some real monsters! Nwanetsi can accommodate 16 people.

Roodewal ★★★

This is the all-round best of the Private camps. Set next to the Timbavati River in the Central Plains, it is smack in the middle of one of the best game-viewing areas in the park. With many tall, shade-giving trees and a relaxed atmosphere, Roodewal is the ideal camp if you want to get away from the rush and bustle of life, and have an abundance of wildlife within easy viewing reach. The camp can accommodate 19 people.

HINT

Air-conditioners are great but they also drown out all other sound. Your room will almost certainly be cool enough by the time you go to bed at night, so turn it off. Most camps, and certainly Satara, have lion in the vicinity and they often roar at night. Listening to the deep-throated roar of a lion in the quiet of night is something you are unlikely to forget. Just hope you have a cooperative neighbour who also has his air-conditioner off!

Best Drives
The Satara/Timbavati River Route ★★★

One of the most game-rich drives in Kruger, this route starts at Satara and proceeds west through a densely-grassed plain filled with tall knobthorn acacias and spreading marula trees. Giraffe and elephant are regular sights here, the vast plain forming a magnificent backdrop for photographing these savanna giants. **Nsemani Dam** is along the way, a favourite drinking point for the herds of zebra and wildebeest which occur abundantly in this area. Lion have learned that many animals congregate here to slake their thirst, so they too base themselves near the dam, and are frequently seen resting in the shade of one of many trees close to the road.

The 61km (38 miles) **S39** gravel route closely follows the meandering path of **Timabavati River**. Take your time along this route; it is a real gem and needs to be savoured slowly in a relaxed frame of mind! The scenery constantly changes back and forth from tall and lush riverine trees to dense combretum woodland and again to open grassland. A short way along this route you'll find the **Piet Grobler Dam** backed by a scenic hill. Animals abound along the entire route; a diverse mix of impala, kudu, giraffe, zebra, wildebeest and a good chance of seeing lion, buffalo, elephant and leopard. Even elusive eland are occasionally spotted.

The **Timbavati Picnic Spot** is about halfway along the S39 road, a convenient spot to walk around and

---

SNAKING SAND

Twisting a path from Orpen camp northwards to its junction with the Olifants River, the Timbavati River is dry for most of the year but its extensive sandy bed suggests that it had substantial flow in earlier times. Despite the negative connotation of the Tsonga term **ku bava** meaning 'bitter or brackish water' from which the river derives its name, the S39 road travelling close to this river is rich in animal life and is one of the best game-viewing drives in the Park.

Below: *Along the scenic Timbavati River is the attractive Piet Grobler Dam named after the grand-nephew of Paul Kruger.*

enjoy a cool-drink or other refreshments. Birds are
plentiful at the picnic spot but perhaps the most
prominent feature associated with this resting area is the
majestic **baobab tree** at the turnoff to the picnic spot. If
you're not going to the far northern areas of Kruger, this
is the place to go to see your baobab tree!

The scenery is especially enjoyable along the second
half of the S39 route. As you approach the area of the
Roodewal Private Camp you will notice the flat-topped
umbrella thorn trees, although most of the best specimens died off during the drought years of the 1980s. In
this same area game is particularly plentiful and you
should see good numbers of zebra, wildebeest and
impala. All too soon you reach the tarred **H1-4** main
road, from where you can either go on to the Olifants
camp or return to Satara. The fun doesn't stop here
though; the routes leading to both these camps also offer
a rich variety of game and beautiful scenery!

The Nwanetsi River to Lindanda Route ★★★

This is yet another excellent route for game-viewing, one
of the top five drives available in Kruger. It takes you
through wonderfully scenic country, one of the best
lookout points in the Park and offers a rich mix of
animals to watch. Try to do this route in the early
morning; the air is refreshing, the photogenic lighting
perfect and the atmosphere at its best.

Below: *The Nwanetsi
River/Lindanda route has
superb game-viewing and is
rated in the top five of the
Kruger's drives.*
Opposite: *The Nwanetsi
Picnic Spot offers breathtaking views of the central
plain rivalled only by those
views at Olifants.*

A highlight for many people is the 19km (12 mile)
S100 gravel road which winds closely next to the
Nwanetsi River, a truly superb drive which offers you
something of everything. Animals are plentiful, birds are
numerous, and the trees lining the mostly dry riverbed
are wonderfully varied, huge Sycamore figs alternating
with stands of magnificently contorted apple-leaf trees.
Nowhere else in Kruger are your chances of seeing a
combination of lion, leopard, buffalo and elephant as
good as here! Even cheetah are occasionally seen during
this drive. Giraffe, impala, zebra and wildebeest are
common, while storks and other waterbirds make excellent photographic subjects as they calmly pose alongside
the quiet pools which dot the riverbed. This route is difficult to beat, especially during the dry winter months
when animals converge nearer the river.

Another major highlight of this route is the **Nwanetsi
Picnic Spot**. Not only does it offer excellent barbecue
facilities adjoining a lovely shaded rest area with tables
and chairs but it has a breathtakingly beautiful lookout
point which is rivalled only by the Olifants camp viewpoint for sheer magnificence! From the shaded seating
of the lookout point you have a huge panoramic view of
the Central Plain, blocked on your left by craggy hills of
the **Lebombo Range**. Eerie *Euphorbia* trees cling to the
stark sides of these hills, reflecting pale green under the

SURVIVING A LION ATTACK

Travelling along the **S35** road
northeast of Tshokwane, you
will reach the Lindanda
memorial site. Lindanda was
the Swazi name for Ranger
Harry Wolhuter, a legendary
figure associated with the
early history of the Kruger
Park. The name is derived
from **lihiya**, a type of loin-
cloth worn by Swazi people,
apparently regularly worn by
Wolhuter in his leisure time.
The memorial site is where
Wolhuter was thrown off his
horse by attacking lions, one
of which dragged him some
distance before the heavily
injured Wolhuter could stab
the animal in the heart. He
then pulled himself into a
tree, waiting there several
hours before tribal assistants
found him and carried him
to hospital over a period of
three days. The knife, a lion
skin and the full story are
exhibited in the Stevenson-
Hamilton Library in Skukuza.

Right: *Orpen Dam is a good place to view animals drinking and to see crocodiles basking in the sun.*
Opposite: *A herd of buffalo cool off at the Kumana Dam along the Satara/Tshokwane route, one of the most game-rich areas in the Kruger.*

hot African sun. Far beneath the lookout point is a large pool in the **Sweni River**, usually with at least one crocodile lying on the rocks. Broad-leaved *Nymphaea* lilies float peacefully on the water, used by graceful Jacana lilytrotters as platforms to search for food. Travelling south along the S37 and S35 roads will take you into another game-rich area. You will be driving parallel to the **Lebombo Mountains** for much of the way, while on your right lies an extension of the enormous Central Plain. It is highly scenic, with lots of wildebeest, zebra, occasional giraffe and a scattering of other species. With just a little luck you may see a beautiful **secretary bird** confidently strutting about the grassy plain, its long, spindly legs exceptionally nimble and used for beating snakes unconscious! The S35 is also known as the **Lindanda road**, a reference to Harry Wolhuter who was very nearly killed by a lion in this area (*see* p. 71). There is a small memorial plaque at the actual site where Wolhuter fought for his life. The countryside here is open grassland, as typically African savanna as you will find described in the most romantic of wildlife books! Near the end of this road you reach **Orpen Dam**, with a hilltop viewpoint where you can get out of the car and admire the view from a shaded seating area. Many animals come here to drink and you can see crocodiles lying in the open. Beyond the dam are picturesque rock-strewn cliffs, an attractive scene with euphorbia trees again visible on the sides.

(*see* p. 71)

FLEET OF FOOT

As serene and peaceful as it may appear, the African savanna constantly applies the rule of 'survival of the fittest'. Nurtured for months inside their mother's womb, a high percentage of antelope calves are born only to succumb to hyena, lion and other predators within hours of entering the harsh open world. To improve their chances of survival, such calves are groggy and disorientated for only a few minutes, after which they can sprint nimble-footed to keep up with the herd and out of danger.

Satara to Tshokwane ★★★

This route combines the comfort of a tarred road withexceptionally good game-viewing opportunities in the most animal-rich area of Kruger. Two enjoyable scenic stops – at Kumana Dam and Mazithi Dam – are well spaced along the route to add 'spice' to the already rich helping of bushveld sights you will encounter along the way. Only a few hundred metres after leaving Satara – shortly before the turnoff to Orpen – you cross the narrow **Shitsakana stream**, dry for most of the year but with a pleasant fringe of lush trees lining the bank. Look carefully into the trees here, it is a favourite spot for leopard to rest! Travelling a short way further, just before the H6 turnoff to Nwanetsi, you cross the **Nwanetsi River**. There is a swimming pool on one side of the bridge, often with a grey stork serenely standing in the water, or buffalo which are common in this area.

The H1-3 road travels through gently undulating open savanna, occasionally becoming somewhat more densely wooded. The uncluttered plain is favoured by cheetah, while the more wooded areas are good for buffalo and elephant. Some 8km (5 miles) before Tshokwane you'll find **Mazithi Dam**, usually with a few waterbuck, wildebeest or other animals in the vicinity. Lion are also regularly seen near this dam, so keep your eyes peeled!

Above: *Along the usually dry Nwaswitsontso River, an area of towering Sycamore figs and lovely green palms.*

Opposite below:
Magnificent Sable antelope, although generally seldomly seen, are often spotted on the Gudzane/Bangu route.

SUPPLE SPEED

The cheetah is the fastest sprinter on land, capable of reaching 100kph (63mph) at full speed. Its acceleration is even more impressive and, in an explosive burst of energy, can reach 70kph (45mph) within three seconds! They cannot sustain these speeds for long though, and soon abandon the chase if the prey is too elusive. Captured prey – usually a small antelope – are choked by biting into the neck.

As you approach Tshokwane picnic site you will be driving parallel to the **Nwaswitsontso River**. Although dry for the greater part of the year, it has a broad sandy bed lined with towering Sycamore figs and broad swaths of intensely green palms which is a highly relaxing and pleasing sight. Tshokwane picnic site is definitely the perfect place for a break after such a richly rewarding and picturesque drive. Enjoy a cup of tea or other refreshments here, stroll around the spacious grounds and watch the numerous fascinating birds for which this picnic spot is so well known!

The Gudzane to Bangu Route ★★

The S90 gravel road travels through Kruger's equivalent of the Serengeti Plains in Tanzania. Rolling fields of tall grass reach to a distant horizon, an occasional gangly tree poking up to provide a resting place for the flocks of birds which inhabit this vast plain. It touches the soul to drive through this enormous flat landscape, a precious treasure of unspoilt Africa welcoming you to enter and enjoy. During the wet summer months the area literally teems with life: a cornucopia of birdlife in all shapes, sizes and colours and herds of wildebeest, zebra and many others. Solitary but spectacularly beautiful lilac-breasted rollers add splashes of colour to the enormous flocks of seed-eating quelea birds, while hundreds of white storks trudge the land or circle the sky, searching for a rich harvest of grasshoppers and other insects.

There are three water-
ing holes which are well
worth spending time at,
as all the herds at some
time wind a path here to
drink their fill. These are
Mavumbye, **Gudzani** and
Bangu. All are situated in
wide open areas excellent
for game-viewing, and
attract herds of zebra,
wildebeest, giraffe and

buffalo. Lion and elephant are regularly seen, and
your chances of seeing the glorious sable antelope are
good. Ostrich are also fairly common in this plain.
To the east, the Lebombo Mountains rise abruptly to
form a thin line on the horizon, a neat fringe to this
idyllic African savanna.

The S90 route between Satara and Balule is only 46km
(29 miles), but will probably take three or four hours to
complete due to frequent stops to watch the animals.
Drive slowly along this route, enjoy and make the most
of the excellent scenery.

Above: *One of the three
watering holes along the
Gudzane and Bangu route
which offer virtually
guaranteed good game-
viewing opportunities.*

AVIAN LOCUSTS

During summer the vast
grassy plains of the Central
District are home to enormous
swarms of seed-eating **red-
billed quelea** birds. As you
drive along the road, especially the S90 near the Bangu
and Gudzane windmills, great
flocks of these nomadic birds
rise from the grass-covered
earth, the tightly-bunched
droves sweeping and swerving
through the air in spectacular
synchrony, a marvellous
display of flight finesse. From
December to April they build
chamber-like nests of
interwoven grass which are
suspended from dense bushes, their massive numbers
attracting many eagles and
other raptors which reap a
rich harvest of nestlings
from the flimsy nests.

5
The Northern Region

Referring to the area between the Olifants River and the Tropic of Capricorn, the Northern Region is dominated by **mopane** trees (*Colophospermum mopane*), a tough, drought-resistant tree. The eastern half – in particular, the enormous stretch between Letaba and Shingwedzi – is a vast, monotonous sea of stunted mopane scrub neatly bounded by the **Lebombo Mountains** on the horizon. Westwards the vegetation changes to a taller, more interesting mix still dominated by mopane, but including large stands of bushwillow (*Combretum apiculatum*) and a liberal sprinkling of gnarled leadwood, apple-leaf, jackalberry and nyala trees. The west also has a sparse but attractive scattering of isolated hills, some of which are rich in **prehistoric artefacts** hinting at long-forgotten lives amid the rock-strewn slopes. The entire region is excellent for viewing **elephant**, while buffalo and zebra are also common. The open mopane scrubland is also the best area in the Park to see **tsessebe**, **ostrich** and, if you are fortunate, also **roan antelope** or **rhino**. **Lion** and **leopard** are regular sights and you may also see **cheetah**.

The best game-viewing and scenery are confined to two fairly distinct areas. The first area is along the Olifants and Letaba rivers, and the other is the area adjoining the Nhlanganini, Ngwenyeni and Tsendze rivers. The **best drives** are along these rivers. Owing to the arid nature of the Northern Region, animals rely heavily on these rivers, which means game concentrations are high and game viewing is very good.

DON'T MISS

*** Letaba Camp: unbeatable atmosphere, wonderful river view, centrally located for game-viewing.
*** Olifants Camp: breathtaking clifftop view of the river and Central Plains beyond.
*** Elephant Hall in Letaba Camp: tusks of the Magnificent Seven, fascinating displays.
** Masorini Hill: archaeological reconstructions of copper smelting communities.
** Engelhardt Dam: home to hippo and sustenance for elephant, buffalo and others.

Opposite: *Impressive tusks form part of the entrance to Olifants Camp.*

Above: *When disturbed caterpillars of the citrus swallowtail inflate a red projection from the head, usually frightening off any predator.*

If you are going to spend a few days in the Northern Region, **Letaba camp** is highly recommended as your base because it is so centrally situated. The camp is a strong favourite with many visitors because of its exceptionally scenic setting along the Letaba River, and the high density of game in the immediate area. Other major camps in the region are Olifants and Mopani, with some smaller camps such as Shimuwini and Boulders.

LETABA ★★★

Strongly recommended as your base camp during your stay in the northern part of Kruger, Letaba is one of the largest and most pleasant camps in the Park, overlooking the Letaba River and densely covered with a highly attractive range of tall trees and palms. The camp lies about 50km (31 miles) east of Phalaborwa midway up the length of the Park, and has close on 340 beds available. There is a large and pleasant camping area with spacious ablution, laundry and cooking units, with ample lush-green lawns on which children can frolic and cavort. You will definitely enjoy the **restaurant,** a real highlight, with its magnificent view over the river. There is a well-stocked **shop** loaded with curios, clothes and other bushveld items tempting you to part with just a little more of your pre-

---

FIELDS OF MOPANE

Much of Kruger north of the Olifants River is dominated by **mopane trees** (*Colophospermum mopane*). The leaves are avidly eaten by elephant, and in most years during December or January, enormous numbers of **mopane worms** (actually caterpillars of the large saturnid moth *Imbrasia belina*) feed on the leaves. These caterpillars are considered a delicacy by local inhabitants, who collect millions of caterpillars in areas adjoining Kruger, spread them in the sun to dry and then either sell them or eat them themselves. It is estimated that during these annual 'outbreaks' the caterpillars eat more mopane leaf-material than elephant in the same area.

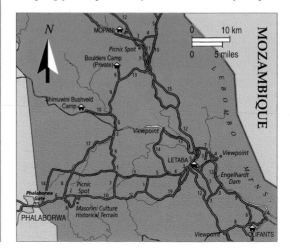

cious store of money! If you're staying in Letaba, or just briefly stopping over, you simply have to visit the **Elephant Hall**, an impressive collection of record tusks and other displays. The sprawling nature of this camp allows you to have some wonderfully enjoyable walks. Birds are plentiful, their variety considerable and their cheerful chirping a constant background presence. You are almost guaranteed to see elephants and other animals coming in for a drink in front of the restaurant. Other facilities in this camp include a **vehicle repair service** (Automobile Association), a **fuel station** and a **cafeteria** which sells a range of pies and other fast-foods which you can enjoy on the verandah with its glorious view.

Highlights of Letaba

Staying in **Letaba** camp is a real pleasure. Make sure you spend some time relaxing on the restaurant verandah, where you can watch elephant, waterbuck and other animals slowly drinking and feeding in the riverbed below. The central location of this camp allows you easy access to the many other attractions in the region. One of the best is the hilltop **lookout point** in front of the Olifants camp restaurant, to many people the **most scenic view in Kruger**. Also a favourite with many visitors is the reconstructed tribal village and iron smelting works at the **Masorini hill** near Phalaborwa. You can spend hours here looking at the various artefacts and taking part in one of the guided tours.

Some **excellent game-viewing drives** radiate from Letaba camp, such as that along the Letaba River to Olifants camp, then along the Olifants River. Another rewarding route is that along the northern bank of the Letaba River to the **Engelhardt Dam** lookout point, or to **Mingerhout Dam**.

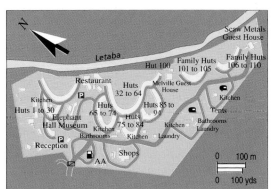

OTHER CAMPS IN THE NORTHERN REGION
Mopani *

Situated midway between Letaba and Shingwedzi, this Main camp is very near the Tropic of Capricorn and straddles a bouldered hill with a grand view over Pioneer Dam. It is a substantial camp catering more for wealthier clients and has about 330 beds. Despite the pleasant layout, modern facilities and many other advantages, the camp has never been a great success and Kruger's management regularly comes up with new attempts to increase occupancy rates. There is nothing wrong with the camp, except that it's hot, with very little shade and you have to drive rather far to get to good game-viewing areas. That aside, it has a very pleasant ladies bar with a magnificent view over the dam, adjoined by a fine restaurant. The entire cafeteria area is on an extensive elevated plankwalk, next to a large and well-stocked shop. Other facilities include a fuel station, swimming pool, conference facilities, launderette, public telephones, but no camping area.

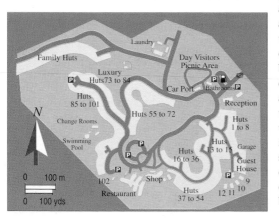

Opposite: *Mopani Camp's restaurant has a fine view over the nearby dam.*
Left: *The spectacular Olifants Camp lookout point above the Olifants River and over the endless plains beyond.*

Olifants **

This Main camp is best known for its spectacular view. Poised high up on the edge of a steep cliff, it offers a panoramic 180° view over the Olifants River far below and the endless plains beyond. Simply magnificent! It is a fairly large camp with about 300 beds but no camping area. The focal point of the camp is the curved sweep made up by the shop, cafeteria and restaurant, leading out to the shaded viewpoint slightly further on. Many huts lie snuggled near the very edge of the cliff giving a magnificent unobstructed view. There is also a conference facility, fuel station, public telephone and launderette. Olifants is close to some of the best game-viewing drives of both the Central and Northern Regions. Best of these are southwards across the Olifants River and into the exceptionally game-rich Central Plains. If it's elephant and buffalo you're after, however, you'd do better travelling the river route north along the Olifants and Letaba rivers to Letaba camp; this route also offers some very scenic viewpoints.

SUGAR LEAVES

A common site in the northern camps and wherever mopane trees occur in Kruger, the curled leaves seen on many of these trees are caused by sap-feeding **mopane bugs** (*Arytaina mopane*). These small insects secrete an off-white, waxy shell for added protection from sun and predators. The waxy shells are sweet and regularly scraped off the leaves by baboons for a tasty snack. The bugs are most common from December to February.

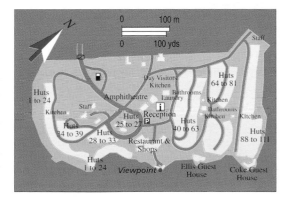

Below: *Pleasant Boulders Private camp has all of its accommodation units raised on wooden pillars, giving elevated views and improved air-circulation.*

Shimuwini **

Pleasantly situated in a scenic setting along the Letaba River near Phalaborwa in quite a remote area, Shimuwini is a firm favourite with many people. The Bushveld camp can take 71 visitors in 15 cottages. Aside from the peaceful and relaxing atmosphere, the main attractions of Shimuwini are the range of birds which can be viewed from camp, and easy access to good elephant and buffalo country and areas frequented by rare sable and roan. The general area surrounding the camp is dominated by a fairly dense cover of mixed mopane and bushwillow.

Boulders *

This pleasant Private camp snuggles against a rocky hill deep in the mopane country of the North, with Mopani as the nearest Main camp where you can buy supplies. The construction style of Boulders differs from the usual serving of 'huts and cottages' available elsewhere in Kruger; all the units are raised high on wooden pillars with plankwalks linking the various units, giving an elevated view and improving air-circulation. If you want to feel a million miles from civilization and undisturbed by faxes, telephones and fretting clients, this is the place to be! Twelve people can be comfortably accommodated in this camp. Game drives in the area are good for seeing tsessebe, zebra, elephant, buffalo, ostrich and others.

BEST DRIVES
The Letaba to Olifants River Route ★★★

Starting at Letaba camp and ending at Olifants camp, the **S46** and **S44** roads closely parallel the two major rivers after which these two popular camps are named. You will have wonderful views of both rivers, including one get out point high on a hill giving you a spectacular vista not only of the rock-studded Olifants River below, but also the pristine bushveld which stretches almost endlessly to converge with the sky in the south and west.

The initial drive along the S46 takes you through some magnificent stands of apple-leaf trees near Letaba camp, interspersed with majestic leadwoods, jackalberries and others. These soon give way to broad fields of mopane trees, where you have an excellent chance of seeing elephant and buffalo. The S46 winds close to the broad bed of the Letaba River and there are many short detours which lead you right to the river's edge. Here you may find waterbuck, elephant, perhaps hippo languishing in the water, and always a variety of birds restlessly romping about the trees.

Within a few hundred metres after turning onto the **S44** you pass through a rocky ridge. Look around carefully for elusive **klipspringer**, a delightful but rare sight restricted to bouldered hills mainly in the southern half of Kruger. They usually perch motionless on a large

---

CROCODILE CARE

The Olifants River has amongst the highest densities of crocodile in Africa. The female lays her eggs in sand, and digs out the hatchling crocodile when warned by their chirping calls. She gently carries her offspring to water and, together with the male, will guard them for several weeks. When eagles or other possible predators approach, the parents aggressively confront the intruder, or vibrate their muscles which warns the young crocodile to dive below water.

Below: *Overlooking the rock-studded Olifants River, home to one of the highest concentrations of crocodile on the African continent.*

rock, their mottled-bronze colour blending well with the surrounds, staring at you with fixed gaze. Superb photographic subjects! The countryside along the **S44** is an arid mix of mopane (*Colophospermum mopane*) and thorny cluster-leaf (*Terminalia prunioides*). With the Lebombo Mountains as an ever-present backdrop often adorned with clusters of *Euphorbia* trees, as well as the occasional view over the river, the scenery is very pleasant.

To top off the already magnificent viewpoints over the Olifants River along the S44 route, the grande finale awaits you in Olifants camp! A short walk from the restaurant verandah takes you to a shaded seating area and a lookout point unequalled elsewhere in Kruger. You are standing on a cliff which drops sheer down to the Olifants River far below, while a stupendous 180° panorama of the Central Plains sweeps to the far-off horizon. A perfect end to your drive!

The Engelhardt Dam Route ***

Probably the most rewarding and enjoyable late-afternoon or early-morning drive available in the Northern Region, this route will take you about two hours to complete and is certain to provide you with lots of memorable sights and scenes. There are two 'legs' to the journey, the first being along the tarred H1-5 road from Letaba camp to the high-level bridge over the

Letaba River. This stretch is a mere 5km (3 miles) but you will be pleasantly surprised by the abundance of wildlife concentrated in this narrow fringe of bush adjoining the Letaba River. The river here for most of the year is a broad expanse of sand, lined by an endless series of footprints and tracks of animals trudging in to the few isolated pools punctuating the scenic riverbed. Elephant dig holes in the sand to reach the clean water below, and you can watch them as they go about their task with slow and deliberate movements. Enormous Sycamore figs line the banks, making it all a very attractive scene. When you reach the high-level bridge, stop close to the side so that you can watch the hippo lolling in the water, periodically surfacing with a great spray of water gushing from the nostrils. While enjoying the view from the bridge, you will no doubt soon become aware of a strong aroma pervading the air! The smell is caused by thousands of free-tailed bats (*Tadarida condylura*) which live in the crevices between the bridge and its supporting pillars.

The gravel S62 forms a short crescent through mopane veld, with several detours leading off to the Letaba River. The river, especially lower down at the Engelhardt Dam, is the only reliable source of water for animals in the region, so they converge here. The short 2km (1.2 miles) detour just before crossing the Makhadzi Spruit is especially rewarding and has loads of pleasant

> **DAMMED SAND**
>
> Located a few kilometres downstream of Letaba camp, funds for the construction of this scenic dam were donated by the American business entrepreneur Charles Engelhardt. From a once strong-flowing river, since the 1970s the Letaba has been reduced to a seasonal river due to the heavy demands on its water by agriculture and towns to the west of the Park. Despite its expanse of water, the Engelhardt Dam is largely silted up and its depth, very shallow.

Opposite: *Only a short walk from the restaurant verandah is the shaded look-out point on a cliff and the Kruger Park's ultimate panoramic view.*
Below: *On the Engelhardt Dam route, hippo congregate in large herds and can be seen lolling in the water.*

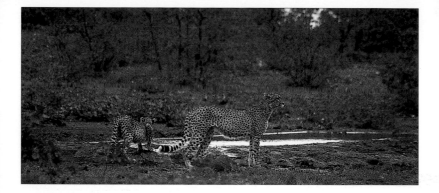

Above: *Cheetah scan the terrain around Nhlanganini Dam, a favourite hunting spot as large herds of game gather here to drink.*

scenery. You'll find kudu here, zebra, impala, perhaps elephant or buffalo, and a wide variety of waterbirds perched in the shallow pools of the Makhadzi or regally poised atop a dead tree along the bank. The S62 finally ends after a sudden climb to a hillside viewpoint where you can get out to enjoy the tranquil scene presented by the substantial Engelhardt Dam and the vast mopane plains all around. Look carefully and you'll see hippo partially submerged near the dam wall!

Letaba to Phalabaorwa Route **

The tarred **H-9** is a somewhat under-appreciated route which has several highlights and attractions. Some 6km (4 miles) from Letaba you cross a narrow creek, very scenic with its granite bed holding placid pools of translucent water. Buffalo often come in to drink here in the late afternoon and the elevated road is an excellent vantage point to watch the jostling animals wade into water. A little further on you'll reach the Nhlanganini Dam, a popular watering hole for herds of buffalo, elephant and a variety of smaller animals and birds. The Nhlanganini River has a narrow bed and only holds water in the wet season but underground water feeds a thin fringe of lush vegetation which stands out from the otherwise rather barren mopane veld. Kudu and giraffe are common along this riverine belt and lion are frequently seen.

NATURAL AIR-CONDITIONING

Large conical termite mounds are conspicuous features over extensive areas of the northern mopane veld. They are made by *Macrotermes* termites, and colonies contain tens of thousands of soldiers, workers and winged reproductives. The enormously enlarged queen and her king lie entombed at the base, near the chambers which house the well-tended fungus gardens which provide the colony with food. Galleries radiate throughout the mound with warm air constantly rising upwards and fresh air entering through thin side-walls.

Shilawuri is an unmistakable landmark between Letaba and Phalaborwa, an isolated but massive outcrop of rocks starkly contrasting with the surrounding mopane plain. Klipspringer occur on this hill but are difficult to photograph. Travelling further west you pass by Erfplaas Windmill and an attractive rocky hill close by the road. This area has rare sable antelope, and rhino too, which often come to drink at the trough served by the windmill. Zebra stir up small puffs of suspended dust as they trudge with nodding heads to the life-giving water.

The highlight of this drive is the stopover at **Masorini Hill**. This is a reconstructed archaeological site well worth a visit. It is one of a series of near pyramid-shaped hills sharply rising from the otherwise blandly level earth. Most of the hills in this area have a rich deposit of artefacts and other signs of previous human habitation, long-disappeared communities which eked out an existence in a harsh environment. At Masorini you can watch and wonder in your mind's eye the activities of these early people, with the comforts of modern life conveniently close at hand! There are toilets here, cool-drinks on sale and barbecue facilities available if you're in the mood.

> ### REKINDLED ASHES
>
> Eleven kilometres (7 miles) from Phalaborwa entrance gate, Masorini Hill stands like a pyramid in an otherwise flat mopane plain. Archaeologists from the University of Pretoria have reconstructed the huts and communal setting of a group of 18th- and 19th-century **Baphalaborwa** ethnic inhabitants. At the foot of the hill, ore was smelted in ovens to extract the iron. This was handed to smithies who worked higher up the hill, refining the crude iron into picks, axes, spears and other implements. These were then traded with dealers for grain and other essentials.

Left: *The reconstructed archaeological site at Masorini Hill, a highlight on the Letaba-Phalaborwa drive. There are refreshment facilities here.*

Above: *The picturesque banks of the Letaba River are often good for spotting elephant and buffalo.*
Below: *Ostriches on the plain near the Malopenyani windmill.*

Letaba to Mopani **

If you own a smart new luxury car and can't face taking it on a gravel road just yet, don't despair! The tarred **H1-6** between Letaba and Mopani will give you a comfortable and dustfree drive, and also surprise you with a good range of animals and sights.

The short stretch between Letaba camp and the Letaba River high-level bridge almost invariably has something interesting to offer, very often elephant feeding on the bank of the broad, sandy riverbed, or drinking at a self-made seephole in the sand. Once on the bridge, look for the portly bodies of hippo wallowing lazily in the pool below, or buffalo resting between the reeds. The broad expanse of sand with a herd of animals strolling across can make a very picturesque photo.

At the junction of the **S48** road with the H1-6, you will see **Malopenyani windmill** slightly to the east of the main road. Very rare indeed is the occasion when you arrive here and there are no animals! It is the only water available in a large area, so animals concentrate here. Rare elsewhere, tsessebe are commonly seen here,

and in fact this is possibly the single most reliable place for you to see tsessebe in the Kruger National Park. Zebra are also common visitors here, as are elephant. Small groups of ostriches roam the vicinity of this windmill, craning their lanky necks to stare in return when visitors stop to watch.

Slightly further north you reach **Middelvlei windmill**, mostly with a stark, barren appearance around the waterhole. This too is a highly favoured waterhole for many animals, hence the heavily trampled environs. Zebra are almost always present, either drinking from the trough, or more often standing around in small groups or rolling in the dust-laden ground. Surprisingly, lion are often seen lying in the shade of one of the many stunted and scraggly acacia trees which punctuate the moonscape.

During the final part of your journey, **Mopani Picnic Spot** presents a welcome break and opportunity to stretch your legs. The picnic site is pleasantly nestled among a grove of unusually big and exquisite-shaped apple-leaf trees, whose shade you will probably welcome by this stage! Buy yourself a cool-drink, then stroll to the thatched viewing area overlooking the **Tsendze River**. Although the river is dry most of the year, there is a semi-permanent pool below the lookout point, regularly used by elephant and buffalo. From here it is a short 15 minute drive to Mopani camp.

Below: *Near the Middelvlei windmill, a zebra rolls in the dust in order to rid itself of ticks and other parasites.*

6
The Far Northern Region

The Far Northern Region extends from the **Tropic of Capricorn** all the way up to the **Limpopo River**, which forms the international border between South Africa and Zimbabwe. A vast sea of mopane trees (*Colophospermum mopane*) dominates most of the area, but fingers of unique sand-associated plant communities push in from the east (the **Wambiya sandveld**) and extreme northwest (the **Punda Maria sandveld**). It is a huge area which is largely arid and flat, but notable exceptions do exist such as around Punda Maria where localized higher rainfall permits the formation of dense groves of tall mopane trees which is the best stand of mature mopane woodland in South Africa! North of Punda Maria, craggy sandstone hills liberally adorn this impressive landscape, made even more memorable by gigantic **baobab trees** which are scattered plentifully throughout the area.

Game-viewing is excellent along the major river-systems of the Region, especially the Shingwedzi/ Mphongolo complex and the Luvuvhu/Limpopo complex. The Far North is by far the best area in the Park for seeing rare **nyala**, **sable**, **roan**, **eland**, and **Lichtenstein's hartebeest**. Elephant and buffalo are abundant, while lion, cheetah and leopard are also regularly seen. The thin fringe of lush riverine woodland adjoining the Luvuvhu River is renowned as an exceptionally rich area for **bird-watchers**, with Pell's fishing owl, Narina trogon, and an exhilarating mix of various robins, bee-eaters, rollers and raptors.

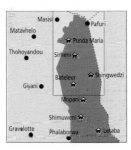

DON'T MISS

*** Shingwedzi Main camp: swimming pool and, close to excellent game-viewing areas.
*** Sirheni bushveld camp: best of Kruger's 'bushveld' type camps, great bird-watching and game-viewing.
*** Mphongolo drive: amongst the top 5 drives.
*** Pafuri: high boabab density, excellent scenery and best bird-watching area.
*** Thulamela archaeological site: artefacts on display.

Opposite: *The huts at Punda Maria, a good base from which to explore the scenic, game-rich Pafuri area.*

CHOCOLATE FLOW

A major tributary of the Limpopo River, the Luvuvhu forms part of the Park's northwestern boundary in the extreme north. It is derived from the Venda tribal name **muvuvhu**, referring to the River Bushwillow tree, *Combretum erythrophyllum*. The Venda name for hippopotamus, **mvuvhu**, is very similar, but apparently is not the origin of the river's name. The drives along this usually chocolate-brown river are highly rewarding, allowing views of several rare birds and animals.

Because of its excellent amenities and proximity to good game-viewing areas, **Shingwedzi** is strongly recommended as a first choice for your base in the Far North. Another good base would be **Punda Maria** which is also a great favourite with many people and offers easier access to the highly scenic and game-rich Pafuri area. Best of all, though, if you don't mind spending just a little extra for the accommodation, is to spend one or two nights in **Sirheni bushveld camp**, a gem of a camp. Sirheni is quite small and as a 'bushveld' type camp has no restaurant or shop, but its wonderful setting, intimate atmosphere and splendid views over a dam hosting an astonishing array of birds makes this camp really worth visiting.

SHINGWEDZI ★★★

Extensive upgrading of Shingwedzi during the 1980s has made this one of the most popular Main camps in Kruger, and it is a camp you should think of visiting on your trip to the Far Northern Region. The various comforts and facilities, together with the increased animal concentrations in the area following the construction of the Kanniedood Dam in 1975, makes Shingwedzi the all-round best camp north of Letaba. It is a large camp which can accommodate some 300 people in huts or cottages and has a big camping ground with ablution blocks and

Below: *Extensively upgraded, Shingwedzi is very popular and has excellent amenities including a lovely pool.*

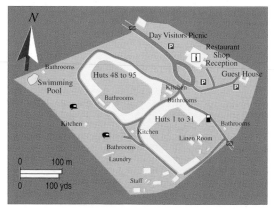

kitchen units. There is a big swimming pool, an enormous reception/shop/restaurant/cafeteria complex and a barbecue area for day-visitors near the entrance gate, overlooking the river. There are several highly recommended drives very near Shingwedzi, such as that along the Kanniedood Dam, the Red Rocks circular drive along the Shingwedzi River, and – best of all – the drive along the Mphongolo River towards Punda Maria. Game concentrations are high along these drives, with the likelihood of seeing elephant, buffalo and many other animals. Shingwedzi is a great camp at which to spend two or three days, then moving on to Sirheni or Punda Maria.

BUSHVELD WINE

One of the most distinctive – and attractive – features of Shingwedzi camp is a clump of unusually tall **Mlala palms** (*Hyphaene natalensis*) towering over the roadway between the shop-complex and the visitors' huts. A common practice in previous years was for local inhabitants to make incisions in the stems of such trees, allowing the sap to drip into a container and then letting the fluid ripen into a powerful, intoxicating broth. Like so many other traditional practices, this habit is also slowly disappearing.

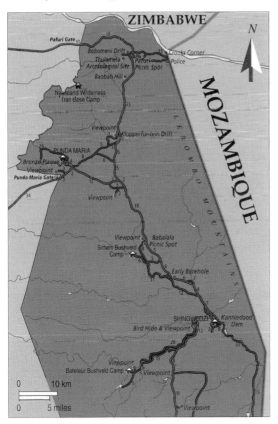

SILENT WITNESS OF HISTORY

Unmistakably distinctive in shape, baobab trees (*Adansonia digitata*) may have a girth of 28m (92ft) or more. Mature trees may be up to 4000 years old. The apparent solid trunk of most boababs is in fact often riddled with large cavities with the entire centre of some trees being hollow. These provide excellent roosting sites for many opportunists, including bats, squirrels, spinetail and other swifts, spiders, scorpions and colonies of bees. A surprising number of these cavities also hold clear pools of water all year round which were a life-saving store of sustenance for many a weary traveller in bygone years.

HILL OF DEATH

Slightly northeast of Punda
Maria, close to the base-
camp of the Nyalaland
Wilderness Trail, extensive
remnants of stone-walls lie
silent atop a high hill overlooking the Luvuvhu valley.
This was the 18th-century
stronghold of **Makahane**,
a chief of the Vhalembethu
tribe. He was widely feared
as a particularly harsh ruler.
Petty offenders were
regularly thrown to their
death over the side of the
cliff. Legend tells of men
being told to stand in a row,
while the chief would parade
nude girls in front of them.
Should any of the men be
aroused, they were to be
thrown over the cliff.
Makahane was eventually
killed by his brother Nelombe
at his father's instruction.

Highlights of Shingwedzi

Shingwedzi is the most popular camp in the Far North.
One of its best attractions is the **swimming pool**, which
in summer always draws crowds seeking respite from
the heat. The spacious and relaxing restaurant/cafeteria
complex has a huge **verandah** which overlooks
the Shingwedzi River and many birds have become
so tame that they fly onto your table in the hope
of easy pickings. Several squirrels are now also getting
into the act. Being a big camp, there are usually enough
visitors to justify **guided day** or **night drives**. Enquire
at the reception office about availability and departure
times. **Game-viewing** is excellent along the several
drives near Shingwedzi, especially along the **Kanniedood Dam** route, the **Red Rocks** route and the
Mphongolo River route.

OTHER CAMPS IN THE FAR NORTHERN REGION
Punda Maria ★★

This is the northernmost camp in Kruger, straddling a
low hill set near the prime baobab country in the Far
North. A big favourite with many visitors, Punda is
a small Main camp offering about 50 beds and an
extensive camping area at the base of the hill with
the usual ablution blocks and kitchen units. The
attractive huts stand on terraces. There is a fuel station,
small shop, restaurant, cafeteria, public telephone
and the 'Paradise Flycatcher Nature Trail'. There are

plans for a swimming pool
adjoining the camping
ground and it should
be available sometime in
the near future. Punda
Maria has a wonderful
atmosphere and is an
excellent base for viewing
magnificent sandstone cliffs
covered with multicoloured
lichen, as well as several of
the rarer animal species.

Bateleur ★★

Bateleur lies southwest of Shingwedzi camp, the surrounding arid country being dominated by mopane and bushwillow trees. The camp is fronted by a dry streambed with lots of tall trees providing shade. During summer a large pool forms in the sandy river, and from the concealed comfort of a hide you can watch animals coming in to drink. The camp can accommodate 34 people and it has a conference room with appropriate facilities. The area around Bateleur is good for viewing some of the rarer animals such as roan, sable and eland, and perhaps even Lichtenstein's hartebeest if you are really lucky.

Sirheni ★★★

Of all the Bushveld camps in Kruger, **Sirheni** is a favourite. It is situated about halfway between Shingwedzi and Punda Maria. It looks out over a dam of the same name and is excellent for a wide range of water birds. The camp has a wonderfully relaxing atmosphere, partly due to the many tall trees, the lack of bustling activity associated with larger camps, and the knowledge that you are in a very remote area of the Park. Whether you're a bird-lover or not, the incredible range and abundance of birds in and around this camp is going to be a marvellous surprise! The herons, geese, storks, jacanas and so many other types strutting and striding around the rippling waters of the dam are simply magnificent. Crocodile lie around lazily on the banks and hippo occasionally break surface with a giant snort and spurt of water, once in a while also venting a series of loud bellows to inform everyone of their presence! Game-viewing is always good along the Mphongolo drive, with excellent chances of seeing game such as nyala, buffalo and elephant. About 80 people can be accommodated.

Above: *The wooden hide at Bateleur Camp offers relaxing opportunities to view an excellent range of birds and nocturnal animals.*

FLYCATCHER NATURE WALK

This trail meanders through some of the wooded areas inside Punda Maria, and is aimed primarily at birdwatchers although anyone would enjoy the great atmosphere and hilltop scenery. Aside from a prized sighting of the beautiful male Paradise flycatcher, you may well also see rare crested guineafowl, with their purple sheen and curly head-dress. Shy bushbuck are regularly seen along the trail, while monkeys gambol about the trees.

Above: *Three kudu cows gather warily to drink at a pool of the Mphongolo River.*

BEST DRIVES
The Mphongolo Route ★★★

This is without doubt the best route in the Far North, and its particular combination of atmosphere, scenery and game richness makes it one of the top three drives anywhere in Kruger. Designated as the **S56** route, it loops and winds close to the edge of the **Mphongolo River**, a major tributary of the Shingwedzi River. During the wet months of summer the river periodically floods and its broad sandy bed is filled with a proud gush of swiftly-flowing water, slowly reduced to isolated pools as winter approaches. Nevertheless these pools are the only sources of water in the area and results in a major concentration of game all along the river. The seasonal flow is also sufficient to support a luxuriant fringe of superb trees and shrubs along the river edge, the profuse foliage and magnificently spreading limbs of the stately trees creating a marvellous atmosphere. Beyond the narrow skirt of riverine lushness, a vast expanse of mopaneveld extends over the flat northern plains, its harsh starkness having a beauty and attraction of its own.

Wildlife abounds along the richly-vegetated edges of the Mphongolo. Buffalo and elephant are common here, either loosely grouped together while feeding lazily on the diverse mix of plants, or eagerly clumped around one of the many pools which dot the serpentine bed of sand.

WHY BURY AN ELEPHANT?

Sirheni is a Tsonga term meaning **at the grave**, said to refer to an elephant which died here of the deadly bacterial disease, anthrax, during the 1959/60 outbreak. He was buried in order to prevent flies and vultures spreading this infectious disease. Outbreaks of anthrax are usually associated with periods of drought, and kill off large numbers of mainly kudu and buffalo. Such outbreaks, however, are normally limited to the North and Far North of Kruger.

Feeding calmly elsewhere in the numerous sun-dappled clearings between clumps of tall trees are regal kudu with their massively spiralling horns, graceful nyala, shy Sharpe's grysbok and many impala. Lion are common here, too, assured of an abundant and select choice of fine prey. Leopard are also regularly seen, the dense riverine vegetation forming their ideal habitat and careful scanning of the trees may reveal a spotted guest.

The vegetation along the river changes constantly, either from clearings patchily dotted with fine-leaved Transvaal mustard bushes, to splendid groves of tall and twisting apple-leaf trees mixed with chequerboard-barked leadwoods, or enormously spreading jackalberries and nyala trees. Numerous little off-roads lead you to better vantage points over the river, or cosy secluded spots where you can stop to watch for birds in the trees. The atmosphere is wonderful, a fairytale land which you have mostly to yourself since relatively few people seem to know about the rewards of travelling this route.

At the end of the S56 road, at its junction with the H1-7 tarred road, you are able to refresh yourself at **Babalala picnic spot**, where cool-drinks are available and also barbecue facilities. Thatched shading built around the trunk of a tall Sycamore fig provides you with a view

> ### THE KILLING FIELDS REPOPULATED
>
> Suffering the same fate as rhino during the late 1800s and early 1900s, **Lichtenstein's hartebeest** were hunted to extinction in their previous northern Kruger National Park home range. In 1985 and 1986 a small core of animals were reintroduced from Malawi and now roam the area between Shingwedzi and Pafuri (another batch near Pretoriuskop). The total number of Lichtenstein's hartebeest in the Park is around 60.

Left: *Buffalo and elephant are abundant in the Mphongolo area.*

PAFURI

One of the most scenic and bird-rich areas of the Park, the name designates that area of the Luvuvhu Valley along the eastern reaches of the river where it flows into Mozambique. Thus there is the Pafuri Picnic Site, Pafuri Border Post and the Pafuri Village in Mozambique.
The term is derived from **Mphaphuli**, a dynastic name of Venda tribal chiefs which ruled the area through which the Luvuvhu River flowed.

Above: *The pristine Pafuri area is exceptionally rich in scenery and wildlife and is especially popular with enthusiastic bird-watchers.*
Below: *Punda Maria is surrounded by the tallest mopane forest in the country and magnificent sandstone koppies.*

over the adjoining veld, or you can stroll around to look at the many birds which frequent the site. Although the S56 is only about 33km (20½ miles) long, you should budget at least three hours for it. It is a route you will definitely enjoy but you need to do it slowly for maximum enjoyment.

Punda Maria to Pafuri ★★★

One of the most remote areas of the Park, the extreme northern tip is nevertheless scenically unsurpassed anywhere else in Kruger: bouldered sandstone ridges and

hills lie scattered throughout the area, while enormous baobabs rise as ageless sentinels from the surrounding mopane plains. Stoically ignoring the harsh heat of the African sun, giant elephant slowly trudge the parched land, scouring bark from baobabs, stripping leaves from mopane, uprooting trees to satisfy a perpetual hunger. The setting is serenely peaceful, undisturbed, Africa at its very best!

Travelling through the mopaneveld towards Pafuri you will pass **Klopperfontein Dam**, a favourite drinking site during the rainy season. Ducks and geese and flocks of various birds frolic here or – like double-banded sandgrouse – pay fleeting visits to quench their thirst before disappearing for another 24 hours. More permanent water is available at **Klopperfontein windmill** and the windmills at **Mazanje** and **Nkovakulu**. Here, daily pilgrimages arrive: elephant, buffalo, zebra and a scattering of smaller animals, all intent on slaking their thirst after a day under a dusty and relentless sun. Lion sometimes watch from the shade of a nearby tall leadwood or jackalberry, while leopard wait for twilight to arrive before venturing from their shady lairs.

Finally, about 8km (5 miles) before you reach the Luvuvhu River, you climb a gentle rise and turn a corner to be confronted by the majestic view of **Baobab hill**. For centuries this tree has poised gracefully atop the rise, solitary guardian to the Livuvhu and Limpopo valleys which stretch beyond. Drive further and you enter the **Pafuri** area, a name which conjures up images of a magic land exceptionally rich in scenery and wildlife to whoever has been here before! Pafuri is indeed almost a sacred word to Park staff, representing a fragile but special ecosystem home to an unusual range of rare birds and other wildlife. Most rewarding in this area are

Above: *Shortly before the Luvuvhu River on the S63 is the majestic Baobab hill, whose guardian for centuries has been this solitary tree.*

> **BVEKENYA – HE WHO SWAGGERS WHEN HE WALKS**
>
> This was the local Tsonga name for Stephanus Cecil Rutgert Barnard, renowned ivory hunter and poacher who based himself in the Pafuri area during the period 1910 to 1929. Police from Mozambique, Zimbabwe and South Africa had warrants for his arrest, but he always managed to evade them. He eventually married, settled on a farm in what is now the North West Province and died in 1962.

the drives which parallel the **Luvuvhu River**. Here you will find magnificent nyala, slow and graceful in their movements. It is the only place in Kruger where nyala are common and they share their special habitat with bushbuck, kudu, buffalo, elephant, impala, baboon and monkeys.

Pafuri is best known throughout the country for its extraordinary rich in birdlife, and so is enormously popular with bird-watchers. The numerous majestically-spreading nyala trees, jackal-berries, Natal mahoganies, Sycamore figs, fever trees and many others form a luxuriant habitat for a multitude of birds which chatter and call incessantly, fluttering about the branches, teasing you to find them. This is where you will find rare Pell's fishing owl, Narina trogon, crested guinea fowl, trumpeter hornbill and a spectacular mix of various robins, bee-eaters, rollers and other birds.

At the wonderfully spacious **Pafuri Picnic Spot** you can relax in the shade of the many giant trees which straddle the Luvuvhu River. You can also buy cool-drinks here and use the barbecue or other cooking facilities that are available. Alternatively, you can simply stroll around admiring the view or keep a watchful eye out for the many facinating birds in this area. Not far from here is the **Thulamela archaelogical site**, a restored 'Zimbabwe Ruins'-type habitation dating back centuries and occupied by a sizable community at one stage.

The Punda or Pafuri trip will undoubtedly turn out to be a highlight of your trip to the Park. Allocate at least seven hours for this trip; you are going to enjoy it and it would be a pity to have to rush it because not enough time was budgeted for it.

CROOK'S CORNER

Wedged between the Luvuvhu and Limpopo rivers in the extreme northeastern corner of the Park, a small triangular tongue of land gained notoriety earlier this century because of the safe haven it offered to various poachers, gun-runners, fugitives and others who were avoiding the law. With no law-enforcers for a great distance, ivory poachers had free rein to hunt in all three countries (South Africa, Mozambique and Zimbabwe). Being conveniently based at the international junction of three countries, it was also quite a simple exercise to cross the border whenever the police of one particular country approached, effectively placing themselves out of the legal reach of those officials.

The Kanniedood Dam Drive ★★★

East of Shingwedzi camp and snuggled intimately close to the **Shingwedzi River**, the first 30km (19 miles) of the **S50** road is widely acknowledged as one of the most enjoyable and rewarding drives of the Far North. The scenery is magnificent, travelling through groves of enormous jackalberry and nyala trees, soaring Sycamore figs and some of the biggest apple-leaf trees to be found anywhere in Kruger. Monkeys and baboons scramble and dash about the branches, disturbing hadeda ibis and many other birds which raucously protest their displeasure at being so rudely chased from their favourite perch.

The **Kanniedood Dam** is along this route, an invigorating expanse of water which serves as a major point of convergence for animals in the area. Herds of elephant and buffalo trundle down the dusty bank for their daily drink, wading in to splash and cool their heated bodies. Crocodile lie silently nearby, instinctively aware that these bulky beasts are to be left alone.

Only a few kilometres from Shingwedzi camp you reach the elevated **bird hide**, a spacious thatch-roofed structure which gives you a comfortably-seated view over the upper reaches of the Kanniedood Dam. During the rainy season when the dam has filled somewhat and many migrant birds have arrived, the area abounds with

> **DIPENE**
>
> Travelling east from Shingwedzi towards the Lebombo Mountains, you reach a small memorial site called **Dipene**. A concrete trough was built here during the major Foot-and-Mouth viral disease outbreak in 1938. All Mozambican migrants moving through this area at the time had to disinfect their feet in this trough. The disease is now known to be endemic in certain wildlife species, with no significant effect to themselves, but poses a major threat to the livestock industry in adjoining farmland outside the Park.

Opposite: *Extensive stonework at the Thulamela archaeological site brings to mind the famous Zimbabwe Ruins, not far from Pafuri.*
Below: *The Kanniedood Dam serves as a major point of convergence for game.*

a fascinating mixture of beautiful and graceful birds. Herons, storks, darters, ducks and geese take their place amid jacanas, wagtails, kingfishers and an almost limitless variety of other smaller birds. The atmosphere here, with all these interesting birds, is simply wonderful!

The best part of the S50 ends at the **Dipene** memorial plaque, where the road veers sharply south away from the river. Here you should decide whether to return to camp or commit yourself to a long drive to Letaba or Mopani.

The Red Rocks Route **

Travelling west from Shingwedzi camp, you reach the **S52** gravel road which closely follows the gentle meanderings of the **Shingwedzi River**. Known as the **Red Rocks** or **Tshanga** road, it takes you through fairly open country which permits easy game-viewing. The dominant feature is the thin line of lush greenness formed by the tall trees which shade the steep banks of the mostly dry Shingwedzi. Concentrated in the vicinity of this line of greenery with its occasional treasure of thirst-quenching water are kudu, impala, zebra, buffalo and a surprising number of elephant. Broken branches stripped of their bark and piles of giant droppings from voided bowels hint at the proximity and abundance of these lumbering hulks.

Adjoining the fringe of riverine vegetation are open patches of veld stubbled by dense **Transvaal mustard** bushes, low shrubby trees with small light-green leaves, often with waterbuck peacefully resting in their shade. Elsewhere the ever-present mopane trees dominate, prime habitat for rare roan antelope and sable.

The S52 crosses the Shingwedzi River near **Tshanga Lookout Point**, not a particularly spectacular viewpoint but nevertheless good bushveld scenery with lots of atmosphere. Lion are regularly seen in this area so keep a sharp lookout!

At the point where you cross the Shingwedzi River there is usually a pool, often with aquatic birds in attendance. Green-backed heron are usually present, standing rigid as a statue ready to strike with their sharp bills at any frog or insect moving within range. Not far from here, near the junction with the H1-6 tarred road, is **Red Rocks Lookout Point**, which gives you a view over the unusual brick-red rock formations in the riverbed. The entire round trip, from Shingwedzi and back, is about 68km (42 miles), a quietly relaxing trip with plenty of wildlife which should take you about four hours to complete.

Opposite: *The mostly dry Shingwedzi River attracts concentrations of game to its few precious pools of water.*
Above: *A young male lion rests in a dry pool near the Tshanga lookout point.*
Below: *Second largest of the Park's antelope is the seldomly seen roan antelope.*

7
Areas Adjoining the Kruger National Park

Situated in the extreme northeastern corner of South Africa, the Kruger National Park is bordered in the north by Zimbabwe, in the east by Mozambique, and for administrative purposes is shared between the North-West Province and Mpumalanga of South Africa. Many visitors driving in to Kruger pass through, or are very near to, some of the most beautiful countryside to be found in South Africa, yet they are unaware of the numerous havens, spectacular sights and experiences which they could enjoy and combine with a visit to Kruger. The **Blyde River Canyon** area is spectacularly beautiful with its many waterfalls, magnificent mountains covered with lush forests, fascinating geological formations sculpted by aeons of erosion, gigantic caves and still-functioning mining villages which vividly portray 19th-century life. All these areas are within close reach of the Kruger Park, making it easy to do combined trips. The routes will take you from the Kruger National Park to the Blyde River Canyon, all the various highlights associated with that region, then on to the famous Pilgrim's Rest mining town and finally along the highly scenic and enjoyable drive to Sabie and Hazyview. Once down the escarpment and into the Lowveld, there are a number of very pleasant **Private Game Reserves**. Quite a number of these reserves have, in fact, become world famous and which pride themselves in providing an unforgettable bush experience combined with maximum luxury and comfort.

DON'T MISS

*** God's Window: a breathtaking view of the lowveld.
*** Pilgrim's Rest: famous gold-mining town.
*** Blyde River Canyon: splendid drive.
*** Mac Mac Falls: the best of a series of magnificent waterfalls in the area of Sabie and Graskop.
*** Private Game Lodges: such as Mala Mala, Londolozi or Sabi Sabi – the ultimate in luxury game-viewing.

Opposite: *The lush green escarpment offers dramatic views and stunning photographic opportunities.*

PRIVATE GAME RESERVES AND LODGES

There are a considerable number of privately-owned game reserves adjoining the western side of Kruger, most of them clustered in the area between Phalaborwa and Hazyview. Most have targeted wealthy, upmarket clients, charging a substantial fee which means that a lot of their visitors are from North America, Europe and the Far East due to the favourable exchange rate. It's very good value for money as most of the lodges offer an excellent package and most guests depart satisfied and

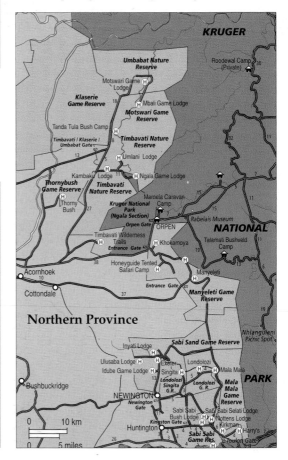

with the best intentions to return again. Typically, the camps and lodges are tastefully constructed, with the emphasis on understated sophistication and luxury. From the outside, the cottages may seem pleasantly rustic and blend well with their bushveld surrounds but inside, every comfort has been thought of to ensure

the maximum enjoyment by the guest. They employ good chefs to prepare mouth-watering meals. At night you usually dine at artistically-arranged settings around a blazing fire, sipping expensive wine from the Lodge's private cellar. The tone is low key. Your hosts never overwhelm you with attention but are discreetly available. Everything is very laid-back, reserved and relaxed, so that no-one feels rushed or pressured at any time.

Typically, guests fly in with **Comair** from Johannesburg to Skukuza, from where you are driven in open Land-Rovers to your particular Reserve or Lodge. You

Above: *Much like the Kruger National Park, private game reserves provide excellent opportunities to view wildlife at close range.*
Below: *Visitors to Mala Mala are virtually guaranteed of the chance to photograph Africa's Big Five.*

MALA MALA

Tsonga for the magnificently beautiful and graceful Sable antelope, Mala Mala covers 18,200ha (45,000 acres) which makes it the largest privately owned 'Big Five' Game Reserve in South Africa. The names Kirkman's Kamp and Harry's Huts are derived from **Harry Kirkman**, a famous ranger who spent most of his life working in the area and had numerous adventures – and sometimes narrow escapes – with lion! Rifles and other paraphernalia used by these early pioneers are displayed in the various camps.

Above: *The courtyard at the now-famous Ngala Game Reserve, where you can dine around a blazing fire sipping excellent wine.*

would have a welcoming drink and time to unpack after which a sumptuous lunch will be served. Then there is time for an afternoon siesta or exploratory walk around the camp, and perhaps a dip in the swimming pool, followed by tea or coffee and refreshments. The highlight is the game drive in the open Land-Rover, escorted by a knowledgeable ranger. All the rangers in a particular area are in radio contact with each other, so if one finds a leopard, the others are notified of its location. They will never allow more than two or three vehicles simultaneously at the site. That would destroy the atmosphere. At dusk the ranger will stop at a scenic spot, unpack the freezer box filled with drinks and will assist you in mixing a drink. Afterwards it's back to camp, with time to bath/shower or otherwise refresh and stroll to the dining area for a relaxing drink and a meal. You will have a choice to join in the early-morning game drive the next day (advisable to do so, well worth it), or to sleep in. After breakfast, many Lodges also offer a **Bushwalk**. Most guests stay for two or three nights before departing again, and some of these Reserves almost guarantee that you will see all the **Big Five** animals (lion, elephant, rhino, buffalo, leopard) during your stay.

Idube Game Reserve ★★

Part of the famous **Sabi Sand** conservation area which embraces most of the other private reserves, Idube has one camp which can accommodate 20 guests in a small but comfortable setting. They offer game-viewing walks and drives in fairly dense bushveld, with lots of birds and wildlife. You can access the reserve by flying in to Skukuza using **Comair**, where you will be fetched, or alternatively you can drive in.

Inyati Game Lodge ★★★

The Lodge has two camps. The Inyati Main camp can accommodate 20 guests in a luxury establishment overlooking the Sand River. It is small and intimate ensuring a memorable stay. The nearby Inyati Treetop Camp is designed for a maximum of 30 guests who come in for the day from hotels or elsewhere in the surrounding areas, departing late afternoon. Inyati means 'buffalo', a reference to the herds of these lumbering beasts with their massively sweeping horns which frequent the area. The lodge has its own landing-strip but many guests fly in to Skukuza with Comair where they are fetched. You can also drive in if you want to.

Londolozi Game Reserve ★★★

One of the 'Big Three' names in private reserves, Londolozi has three camps, all of which closely adjoin each other and overlook the broad bed of the Sand River. **Main Camp** accommodates 24 guests, **Bush Camp** 16 people, and **Tree Camp** 8 guests. People from all over the world have come to know Londolozi as a 'value for money' experience, spreading the word to their friends about the high quality of relaxation, comfort and game-viewing which is to be experienced in the privacy of this well-managed reserve. An excellent adventure awaits you here! Londolozi even has its own landing-strip, or if you prefer you can fly in to Skukuza with **Comair**, from where you will be flown to the reserve in a much smaller aircraft. Alternatively, you can also drive in.

A Gift to All
Ngala (Tsonga for lion) Game Reserve owes its existence to the generous donation of 15,000ha (37,000 acres) of privately owned land to the National Parks Board by philanthropist Hans Hoheisen. The National Parks Board established a 'contract reserve' with the **Conservation Corporation** in 1990, thus combining the wildlife management skill of the National Parks Board with tourism expertise of Conservation Corporation.

Below: *For some of the ultimate in leopard viewing, go on a game drive through Londolozi Game Reserve.*

Above: *Mala Mala Game Reserve, renowned as one of the worlds best tourist destinations, offers sophistication and superb game-viewing.*

Mala Mala
Game Reserve ★★★

This is probably the best known of all the private reserves and is favoured by the world's rich and famous because of the combination of privacy, discretion and high sophistication. Reputed to be one of the world's 'Top Ten' resorts, it has four camps. **Main Camp** accommodating 50 guests, **Kirkman's Camp** 20 people, **Kirkman's Cottage** 8 guests, and **Harry's Camp** 14 people. Mala Mala guests are treated to the best of what is offered by the private game reserves and you will undoubtedly have an exciting and highly enjoyable African experience in this game-rich paradise. Prices are steep but it is likely to be an unforgettable holiday with lifelong memories. Access to Mala Mala is mostly via Skukuza using **Comair** from Johannesburg, or you can drive in.

Ngala Game Reserve ★★★

Another first class resort operated by the highly professional Conservation Corporation, Ngala is located near Orpen Gate and has one camp – **Ngala Lodge** capable of accommodating 42 guests. Guests are treated to excellent accommodation, cuisine, comfort and service. **Ngala** means 'lion' which happen to be abundant in this game-rich part of the Lowveld. The reserve straddles several vegetation zones, most noticeably the unmistakable mopaneveld which covers vast areas further north and the beautiful Timbivati flood plains, all with their own unique mix of plants, birds and animals. Lots to keep you fascinated! Access to Ngala is with **Comair** from Johannesburg to Skukuza and then by private aircraft to the Lodge. Alternatively, you can drive in.

ECHO CAVES

Gouged from the bowels of a dolomite ridge near the town of Ohrigstad, these caves derive their name from the echoes which result when tapping the numerous stone formations. In ages past the place served as a refuge for African tribes, and many Stone Age and Iron Age relics have been recovered from the caves. These are all described and depicted in the open-air Museum of Man.

Sabi Sabi Game Reserve ★★★

This is a well-established and well-known reserve, highly regarded internationally for a sophisticated and quality 'African Experience'. It has three camps, **Bush Lodge** which accommodates 54 guests, **River Lodge** 48 guests and **Selati** 14 guests. The reserve is conveniently close to the Skukuza airport, so that most guests fly in from Johannesburg using **Comair**, although you can drive in if you prefer. The Sabie River forms part of the boundary of this reserve, a river which is well known for the high diversity of birds which frequent the tall trees and lush growth adjoining the river. Game is particularly plentiful here too and you have an excellent opportunity of seeing all the 'Big Five'!

Singita Game Reserve ★★★

Small and intimate, **Singita** means 'The Miracle' and is a relatively new addition to the Conservation Corporation's several reserves in the area. It has a single, luxury lodge which accommodates 16 guests in magnificent style and comfort, with food and wine of exceptional quality. The lodge was once a hunting camp and is set in one of the prime game-viewing areas in the Lowveld. This is one of the finest bush experiences in Africa, guaranteed to give you a memorable stay! Access to Singita is through Skukuza airport using **Comair** from Johannesburg or else you can drive in.

BOOMTOWN MEMORIES

Discovery of gold in 1873 brought prospectors and adventurers flocking to **Pilgrims Rest**. Despite other gold rushes to Barberton and later the 'Big Daddy' of all – the Witwatersrand, Pilgrims Rest flourished and gold continued to be mined there until 1972. Now the town is a well-preserved 'living museum' and the main street is virtually unchanged from a century before. The town and its shops rely heavily on tourism for income. There are many fascinating displays, curio shops, artists' outlets and cottage industries.

Below: *A wooden leisure deck overlooking a watering hole in Singita Game Reserve, a wonderful new luxury lodge.*

Below: *The dramatic Blyde River Canyon, one of Africa's great natural wonders.*

UluSaba **

Tucked into the northwest corner of the Sabi Sand Conservation Area, Ulu-Saba is another exclusive reserve offering imaginative and sophisticated comfort and cuisine. It has two camps, **Rock Lodge** which accommodates 24 guests in a unique hilltop setting having a spectacular panoramic view of the surrounding bushveld, and **Safari Lodge** which caters for 10 visitors. The management pride themselves in providing an outstanding service, aiming to exceed your greatest expectations. Access to the reserve is either by flying in to Skukuza with **Comair** from Johannesburg, or driving in.

THE ESCARPMENT

Kruger and the adjoining broad strip of land on its western side form a vast bushveld plain bordered in the east by the Indian Ocean and in the west by the sharply defined Drakensberg escarpment. This escarpment region, a zone of rapidly increasing altitude, has been planted extensively with pines and other commercial trees, but urban and other scenically destructive development has been minimal. This, combined with higher annual rainfall than that in the lower-lying bushveld plains, has resulted in often breathtakingly beautiful scenery which rivals the beauty even of the Western Cape and Garden Route. Excellent access to the area is available through wide, well-maintained tarred roads which wind their way between and over the mountainous terrain and lush forests which cover much of the hillsides. Various lookout points allow you to admire the sometimes stunning view such as at God's Window, Wonder View, Kowyn's Pass and numerous other places along the various roads traversing the area. There are

---

DOING IT BY TRAIN

Said to be 'the most luxurious train in the world', **Rovos Rail's Pride of Africa** regularly travels between Pretoria and Komatipoort as part of it's broader network of tours. It is a privately owned, beautifully restored Edwardian train guaranteeing you utter luxury, comfort and security. From Komatipoort you can take a rental car into the Kruger National Park and the adjoining attractions of the escarpment.

other attractions too, such as superb waterfalls which cascade over vertical drops and rival the beauty of most waterfalls anywhere in the world. Most accessible of these is the Mac Mac Fall between Sabie and Graskop, an unforgettable sight in a magnificent setting!

Other waterfalls abound in the area and can be reached by taking short detours off the main roads. Best known are the Lisbon Falls, Bridal Veil Falls, Sabie Falls, Forest Falls and Lone Creek Falls but there are many others. Equally fascinating are the many geological formations which nature has twisted, gouged and shaped over millions of years. Most worthwhile visiting are the Sudwala caves between Nelspruit and Lydenburg, where the cavernous cavities sometimes host symphony orchestras, or the Echo caves near Ohrigstad. Other fascinating natural features are the Bourke's Luck Potholes, huge artistically eroded holes scoured into rock and the massive Blyde River Canyon, one of the most scenic areas in Africa. But it's not all just natural beauty! There are also quaint roadside stalls selling handicraft, curios and fruit, 'living museums' such as the perennially popular Pilgrim's Rest village with its intriguing souvenir shops. This pioneering town of the raucous goldmining era still retains a glimmer of the adventurous atmosphere of bygone days and has an endless variety of locally made handicraft and other paraphernalia on sale. Spread throughout the escarpment are numerous hotels and pleasure resorts discreetly tucked away so as not to disturb the scenery along the various routes and they offer a multitude of fun pastimes including horse-riding, walking trails, canoeing, fly-fishing, swimming, helicopter rides, golfing, or simply a relaxed atmosphere where you can unwind in magnificent surrounds.

Below: *The Lisbon Falls, just one of the many scenic attractions which abound in the Kruger area.* **Overleaf:** *King of the beasts, the splendidly maned male lion is the top attraction in the game lodges and parks.*

The Kruger National Park At a Glance

BEST TIMES TO VISIT

Anytime really as each season has its own highlights. **Game-viewing** is best during the dry winters because trees have dropped their leaves, the grass-cover is less and animals are forced to visit the few remaining waterholes. Many people prefer the cooler temperatures of winter, and the malaria risk is negligible. For overall atmosphere, the **wet season** (November – February) is best since flowers abound, lush growth of grass and trees has a definite beauty, many animals calve or lamb at this time, and summer bird migrants arrive. But the **malaria** risk is higher and it gets very hot. If you have only two or three days and want to see maximum game, visit in July/August.

GETTING THERE

The southern half of Kruger is the most popular and access is either by air or road. **Comair**, tel: (011) 921-0222 or 921-0111. There are daily scheduled flights between Johannesburg and Skukuza. Comair also offers various tours around the southern half of the Park. This can include visits to areas adjoining the Kruger Park if you like, and can be arranged through the same numbers listed above.

Avis Rent-a-car: There is a branch in Skukuza,

tel: (01311) 65651.
If **travelling by car** from the Johannesburg/ Pretoria area, the quickest access to **Skukuza** or the **southern KNP** is via Witbank, Belfast, Nelspruit, White River, Hazyview and Kruger Gate. As an alternative, a more scenic route, only one or two hours longer, is via Witbank, Belfast, Dullstroom, Lydenburg, Sabie, Hazyview and Kruger Gate. For the **central region** of Kruger travel via Witbank, Belfast, Nelspruit, White River, Hazyview, Acornhoek then Orpen Gate. To reach the **northern parts** of Kruger, travel via Pretoria, Naboomspruit, Pietersberg, Tzaneen and Phalaborwa. For the **extreme north** go via Pretoria, Naboomspruit, Pietersburg, Louis Trichardt and Punda Maria.

GETTING AROUND

Avis is the only rental agency with a branch in Kruger. They have an office at the Skukuza Airport and Skukuza Reception Office, tel: (01311) 65651, central reservations, tel: 0800 21111. They will deliver vehicles at any point you wish, virtually anywhere in the Park.
Bush Drives: These are educational daytime drives in Parks Board vehicles with experienced guides, and are available from Skukuza, Berg-

en-Dal and Letaba. A maximum of seven people can be taken per trip, which lasts three or four hours. Reservations have to be made in advance at the **Environmental Education Centre** in Skukuza, tel: (01311) 65611 (ask for extension 2340). Animals are more active in the early morning and late afternoon, and your chances of seeing game are improved during those times. During the mid-day heat most animals will rest in the shade, remaining quite still which makes them difficult to see.

WHERE TO STAY

Kruger has 24 camps offering a very wide selection of accommodation, from multi-roomed luxury houses down to furnished tents, or camping grounds where you can pitch your own tent or park your mobile home. Two- or three-bed huts or rondavels are the standard type of units, the majority having their own shower and toilet and are available with or without kitchenettes. Remember that during the school holidays which are the months of April, July and December, as well as long weekends, the number of casual day visitors to the Park is limited and accommodation is often very difficult to obtain.

The Kruger National Park At a Glance

RESERVATIONS
Pretoria
tel: (012) 343-1991
fax: (012) 343-0905.
Cape Town
tel: (021) 22-2810
fax: (021) 24-6211.
Skukuza
tel: (01311) 65159
(08:00–17:30 or 18:00).
Office hours: 08:00–15:45
(Skukuza and Pretoria)
09:00–16:45 (Cape Town).

MAIN CAMPS
Conference facilities:
Available at Berg-en-Dal, Jakkalsbessie, Bateleur and Mopani. Reservations are to be made through the Pretoria head office, at fax: (012) 343-2006.

Balule (satellite of Olifants), tel: (01311) 66606/7.
Berg-en-Dal, tel: (01311) 66106/7.
Crocodile Bridge, tel: (01311) 66012.
Letaba, tel: (01311) 6636/7.
Lower Sabie, tel: (01311) 66056/7.
Marula (satellite of Orpen), tel: (01311) 66355.
Mopani, tel: (01311) 66536.
Olifants, tel: (01311) 66606/7.
Orpen, tel: (01311) 66355.
Pretoriuskop, tel: (01311) 65128.
Punda Maria, tel: (01311) 66873.

Satara, tel: (01311) 66306/7.
Shingwedzi, tel: (01311) 66806/7.
Skukuza, tel: (01311) 65159.
(**Balule** and **Marula** camps do not have their own Reception Offices or telephone numbers; they have to be contacted via **Olifants** and **Orpen**, respectively).

BUSHVELD CAMPS
Bateleur, tel: (01311) 66843.
Biyamiti, tel: (01311) 66171.
Jackalsbessie, tel: (01311) 65490.
Shimuweni, tel: (01311) 66683.
Sirheni, tel: (01311) 66860.
Talamati, tel: (01311) 66343.

PRIVATE CAMPS
None of these private camps have Reception Offices so reservations have to be made through the **National Parks Board Regional Offices** at Skukuza, tel: (01311) 65159.
Boulders
Jock of the Bushveld
Malelane
Nwanetsi
Roodewal

PRIVATE GAME RESERVES
Idube Game Reserve
tel: (011) 888-3713
fax: (011) 888-2181.

Inyati Game Lodge
tel: (011) 493-0755
fax: (011) 493-0837.
Londolozl
tel: (011) 803-8421
fax: (011) 803-1810.
Mala Mala
tel: (011) 789-2677
fax: (011) 866-4382.
Ngala Game Reserve
tel: (011) 803-8421
fax: (011) 803-1898.
Sabi Sabi
tel: (011) 483-3939
fax: (011) 483-3799.
Singita
tel: (011) 803-8421
fax: (011) 803-1898.
UluSaba
tel: (011) 465-4240
fax: (011) 465-6649.

HOTELS
LUXURY
Casa do Sol
(Hazyview)
tel: (01317) 68111.
Cybele Forest Lodge
(White River)
tel: (01311) 50511.
Mount Sheba
(Beyond Pilgrim's Rest)
tel: (011) 788-1258/9.

MID-RANGE
The Farmhouse Country Lodge
(Hazyview)
tel: (01317) 68780.
Jatinga Country Lodge
(Nelspruit)
tel: (01311) 31932.
Karos Lodge
(Outside Kruger Gate)
tel: (01311) 65671.

The Kruger National Park At a Glance

Malelane Lodge
(Malelane)
tel: (01313) 30331.
Pine Lake Sun
(White River)
tel: (01311) 31186.
Sabi River Sun
(Hazyview)
tel: (01317) 67311.
The Winkler
(White River)
tel: (01311) 32317.
Bohms Zeederberg
(Hazyview)
tel: (01317) 68101.
The Crocodile Country Inn
(Nelspruit)
tel: (01311) 63040.
Promenade Hotel
(Nelspruit)
tel: (01311) 53000.
Blue Mountain Lodge
(Hazyview)
tel: (01317) 68446.

BUDGET
Hazyview Protea Hotel
(Hazyview)
tel: (01317) 67332.
Hotel Numbi
(Hazyview)
tel: (01317) 67301.
Paragon Hotel
(Nelspruit)
tel: (01311) 53205.
Blyde Lodge
(Graskop)
tel: (01315) 71316.
Fig Tree Hotel
(Nelspruit)
tel: (01311) 53201.
Graskop Hotel
(Graskop)
tel: (01315) 71244.

Karula Hotel
(White River)
tel: (01311) 32277.
Protea Floreat Hotel
(Sabie)
tel: (01315) 42160.
Royal Hotel
(Pilgrim's Rest)
tel: (01315) 81100.
Sabie Valley Inn
(Sabie)
tel: (01315) 42182.
Sanbonani Lowveld Hotel
(Hazyview)
tel: (01317) 67340.
Town Lodge
(Nelspruit),
tel: (01311) 41444.

SELF-CATERING
Aventura Blydepoort
(Blyde River Canyon)
tel: (01323) 80155.
Crystal Springs Mountain Lodge
(Pilgrim's Rest)
tel: (01315) 81153.
Eagles Nest Chalets
(Hazyview)
tel: (01317) 67021.
Fern Tree Park
(Sabie)
tel: (01315) 42215.
Hazyview Farm Cottages
(on private farms in Hazyview),
tel: (011) 9753017.
Kruger Park Lodge
(Hazyview),
tel: (01317) 67021.
Log Cabin Village
(Graskop)
tel: (01315) 71974.
Trout Hideaway
(Pilgrim's Rest)
tel: (01315) 81347.

Berg-en-Dal, Letaba, Lower Sabie, Mopani, Olifants, Pretoriuskop, Punda Maria, Satara, Shingwedzi and Skukuza have restaurants and fast-food cafeterias. The camp restaurants are all fully licenced and serve a wide range of wines and other refreshments.

Hippo Hollow
(Hazyview)
tel: (01317) 67752.
Loggerhead Restaurant
(Sabie)
tel: (01315) 43341.
Porterhouse Steakhouse
(Nelspruit)
tel: (01311) 26951.
Arkansas Spur Steak Ranch
(Nelspruit)
tel: (01311) 23619.
Tembi Restaurant
(Hazyview)
tel: (01317) 67729.
Timbuctoo Restaurant
(White River)
tel: (01311) 33353.
Villa Italia
(Nelspruit)
tel: (01311) 25780.

TOURS AND EXCURSIONS

Comair offers combined Fly-in or Travel Tours inside the Kruger National Park and visitors are accompanied by experienced guides. For further information on the facilities available, tel: (011) 921-0222, (011) 921-0111 or (01311) 65644.

The Kruger National Park At a Glance

Bushveld Breakaways,
PO Box 926,
White River 1240,
tel: (01311) 51998,
fax: (01311) 50383.
Bushveld Experience,
PO Box 2226,
Primrose 1416,
tel: (011) 828-2362.
Comair Safaris,
PO Box 7015,
Bonaero Park 1622,
tel: (011) 921-0209,
fax: (011) 973-1659.
**Clive Walker Trails
and Safaris**,
PO Box 645,
Bedfordview 2008,
tel: (011) 453-7645,
fax: (011) 453-7649.
Drifters,
PO Box 48424,
Roosevelt Park 2129,
tel: (011) 888-1160,
fax: (011) 888-1020.
**Indabushe Tours
and Safaris**,
PO Box 275,
North Riding 2165,
tel/fax: (011) 888-1246.
Welcome Tours & Safaris,
P.O.Box 2191,
Parklands 2121,
tel: (011) 442-8905,
fax: (011) 442-8865.
Wilderness Safaris,
PO Box 651171,
Benmore 2010,
tel: (011) 884-1458,
fax: (011) 883-6255.

USEFUL CONTACTS

For information about areas
adjoining Kruger, such as
accommodation, **safaris**

and **game drives**, **river
rafting**, **hiking trails**,
hot air ballooning, or
other tours and excursions
and general advice, contact
the following organizations:
Nelspruit Publicity Office,
tel: (01311) 551988.
**Sondela Tourist
Information**
(Sabie)
tel: (01315) 43492.
**Lydenburg Tourist
Information**,
tel: (01323) 2121.
**Graskop Tourist
Information**,
tel: (01315) 71244.

For information about South
Africa's national parks, contact
the National Parks Board at
its various offices:
Pretoria Head Office,
PO Box 787,
Pretoria 0001,
tel: (012) 343-1991,
fax: (012) 343-0905; or
Cape Town Office,
PO Box 7400,
Roggebaai 8012,
tel: (021) 22-2810,
fax: (021) 24-6211.
For reservations in Kruger
and general information,
contact the **Skukuza Office**,
tel: (01311) 65159.

CROCODILE BRIDGE	J	F	M	A	M	J	J	A	S	O	N	D
AVERAGE TEMP. °F	80	79	77	73	66	60	60	64	70	7	76	79
AVERAGE TEMP. °C	27	26	25	22	19	16	16	18	21	3	24	26
HOURS OF SUN DAILY	7	8	7	7	8	8	8	8	8	2	6	7
RAINFALL ins.	4	4	3	2	1	0.5	0.5	0.5	1	3	3	3
RAINFALL mm	107	102	66	43	18	11	9	8	23	7	77	87
DAYS OF RAINFALL	7	7	7	4	2	2	1	3	3	2	7	7

SATARA	J	F	M	A	M	J	J	A	S	O	N	D
AVERAGE TEMP. °F	80	80	77	73	66	63	60	66	70	76	76	79
AVERAGE TEMP. °C	27	27	25	23	19	17	16	19	21	24	24	26
HOURS OF SUN DAILY	7	8	7	7	8	8	8	8	8	7	6	7
RAINFALL ins.	2	4	2	1	0.5	1	0.5	0.5	1	2	2	3
RAINFALL mm	51	91	42	25	7	15	8	9	16	38	59	76
DAYS OF RAINFALL	9	7	5	4	2	2	1	2	2	4	7	7

PRETORIOUSKOP	J	F	M	A	M	J	J	A	S	O	N	D
AVERAGE TEMP. °F	77	77	75	70	66	63	60	66	70	70	73	75
AVERAGE TEMP. °C	25	25	24	21	19	17	17	19	21	21	23	24
HOURS OF SUN DAILY	7	8	7	7	8	8	8	8	8	7	6	7
RAINFALL ins.	4	4	3	2	1	1	1	1	1	2	4	4
RAINFALL mm	111	103	76	56	22	17	17	13	16	57	103	99
DAYS OF RAINFALL	10	8	6	7	3	3	2	2	3	8	12	10

Wildlife Checklist

MAMMALS
Antelope
  Bushbuck
  Duiker, common or grey
  Eland
  Grysbok, Sharpe's
  Impala
  Klipspringer
  Kudu
  Nyala
  Reedbuck
  Roan
  Sable
  Steenbok
  Tsessebe
  Waterbuck
  Wildebeest, blue
  Zebra, Burchell's
Baboon, chacma
Bats
Buffalo, African
Cats
  Caracal
  Cheetah
  Leopard
  Lion
  Serval
  Wild cat, African
Civet
Elephant
Genet
Giraffe
Hare
Hippopotamus
Hyena, spotted
Jackal, black-backed
Mongoose, banded
  dwarf
Monkey, vervet
Rhinoceros, black
  white
Rodents
  Mouse
  Porcupine
  Rat, black house
Springhare
Squirrel, tree
Warthog
Wild-dog
Zebra *see* antelope

BIRDS
Bateleur *see* Eagle
Bee-eater, carmine
  European
  little
  white-fronted
Bishop, golden
  red
Bulbul, black-eyed
Bustard, Kori
Crane, black
Darter
Dikkop, spotted
  water
Dove, Cape turtle
  emerald-spotted
  laughing
  red-eyed turtle
Duck, knob-billed
  white-faced
Eagle, African fish
  bateleur
  brown snake
  martial
  tawny
  Wahlberg's
Egret, cattle
Francolin, coqui
  crested
  Natal
  Shelley's
  Swainson's
Goose, Egyptian
  spur-winged
Goshawk, little banded
Guinea-fowl, crested
  crowned
Hamerkop

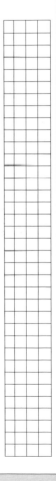

Wildlife Checklist

Helmet shrike, red-billed		
white		
Heron, goliath		
green-backed		
great white		
grey		
Hornbill, crowned		
grey		
ground		
red-billed		
trumpeter		
yellow-billed		
Ibis, hadeda		
Jacana, African		
Kingfisher, brown-hooded		
giant		
grey-hooded		
half-collared		
malachite		
pied		
pygmy		
striped		
woodland		
Korhaan, black-bellied		
red-crested		
Loerie, grey		
purple-crested		
Nightjar		
Ostrich		
Owl, Pel's fishing		
Oxpecker, red-billed		
yellow-billed		
Parrot, brown-headed		
brown-necked		
Plover, blacksmith		
crowned		
Quelea, red-billed		
Roller, European		
lilac-breasted		
Ruff		
Sandpiper, common		
wood		
Starling, Burchell's glossy		
Cape glossy		
plum-coloured		

red-winged		
wattled		
Stork, black		
marabou		
open-bill		
saddlebill		
white		
white-bellied		
woolly-necked		
Sunbird, Marico		
Swallow, lesser striped		
Vulture, Cape		
Egyptian		
hooded		
lappet-faced		
white-backed		
white-headed		
Weaver, Cape		
golden		
masked		
red-headed		
spectacled		
spotted-backed		
Widow, Cape		
long-tailed		
white-winged		

REPTILES

Crocodile, Nile		
Lizards		
Agama, tree (black-necked)		
Chameleon,		
common East African		
(flap-necked)		
Gecko		
Leguaan		
Snakes		
Cobra, Egyptian (banded)		
Mozambique		
(black-necked) spitting		
Mamba, black		
Puff adder, African		
Python, African		
Tortoises and Terrapins		